SEVEN PLAYS OF THE SEA

EUGENE O'NEILL

SEVEN PLAYS
OF THE SEA

VINTAGE BOOKS

A Division of Random House   New York

VINTAGE BOOKS EDITION, NOVEMBER 1972

Copyright 1919 by Eugene O'Neill
Copyright renewed 1947 by Eugene O'Neill

All rights reserved under International and Pan-American
Copyright Conventions. Published in the United States by
Random House, Inc., New York. Distributed in Canada by
Random House of Canada Limited, Toronto. Originally
published by Horace Liveright in 1919 and by Modern
Library in 1922.

Library of Congress Cataloging in Publication Data

O'Neill, Eugene Gladstone, 1888–1953.
Seven plays of the sea.   172930

First published in 1919 under title: The moon of the
Caribbees, and six other plays.

I. Title.   [PS3529.N5M7 1972]   812′.5′2   72–4167
ISBN 0–394–71856–9

Manufactured in the United States of America
B987654321

CONTENTS

THE MOON OF THE CARIBBEES

A Play in One Act

CHARACTERS

Seamen of the British tramp steamer Glencairn

YANK	SMITTY
DRISCOLL	PAUL
OLSON	LAMPS, *the lamptrimmer*
DAVIS	CHIPS, *the carpenter*
COCKY	OLD TOM, *the donkeyman*

Firemen on the Glencairn

BIG FRANK	MAX
DICK	PADDY

West Indian Negresses

BELLA	VIOLET
SUSIE	PEARL

THE FIRST MATE

Two other seamen—SCOTTY AND IVAN—and several other members of the stokehole-engine-room crew.

NOTE With the exception of "In the Zone," the action of all the plays in this volume takes place in years preceding the outbreak of the World War.

THE MOON OF THE CARIBBEES

SCENE   *A forward section of the main deck of the British tramp steamer* Glencairn, *at anchor off an island in the West Indies. The full moon, half-way up the sky, throws a clear light on the deck. The sea is calm and the ship motionless.*

    On the left two of the derrick booms of the foremast jut out at an angle of forty-five degrees, black against the sky. In the rear the dark outline of the port bulwark is sharply defined against a distant strip of coral beach, white in the moonlight, fringed with coco palms whose tops rise clear of the horizon. On the right is the forecastle with an open doorway in the center leading to the seamen's and firemen's compartments. On either side of the doorway are two closed doors opening on the quarters of the bosun, the ship's carpenter, the messroom steward, and the donkeyman—what might be called the petty officers of the ship. Near each bulwark there is

*also a short stairway, like a section of fire
escape, leading up to the forecastle head (the
top of the forecastle) —the edge of which can
be seen on the right.*

*In the center of the deck, and occupying
most of the space, is the large, raised square
of the number one hatch, covered with can-
vas, battened down for the night.*

*A melancholy negro chant, faint and far-
off, drifts, crooning, over the water.*

*Most of the seamen and firemen are reclin-
ing or sitting on the hatch.* PAUL *is leaning
against the port bulwark, the upper part of
his stocky figure outlined against the sky.*
SMITTY *and* COCKY *are sitting on the edge of
the forecastle head with their legs dangling
over. Nearly all are smoking pipes or cigarettes. The majority are dressed in patched
suits of dungaree. Quite a few are in their
bare feet and some of them, especially the
firemen, have nothing on but a pair of pants
and an undershirt. A good many wear caps.*

*There is the low murmur of different con-
versations going on in the separate groups as
the curtain rises. This is followed by a sudden
silence in which the singing from the land
can be plainly heard.*

DRISCOLL [*A powerfully built Irishman who is
sitting on the edge of the hatch, front—irritably*]
Will ye listen to them naygurs? I wonder now, do
they call that keenin' a song?

SMITTY [*A young Englishman with a blond mustache. He is sitting on the forecastle head looking out over the water with his chin supported on his hands*] It doesn't make a chap feel very cheerful, does it? [*He sighs.*]

COCKY [*A wizened runt of a man with a straggling gray mustache—slapping* SMITTY *on the back*] Cheerio, ole dear! Down't be ser dawhn in the marf, Duke. She loves yer.

SMITTY [*Gloomily*] Shut up, Cocky! [*He turns away from* COCKY *and falls to dreaming again, staring toward the spot on shore where the singing seems to come from.*]

BIG FRANK [*A huge fireman sprawled out on the right of the hatch—waving a hand toward the land*] They bury somebody—py chiminy Christmas, I tink so from way it sound.

YANK [*A rather good-looking rough who is sitting beside* DRISCOLL] What d'yuh mean, bury? They don't plant 'em down here, Dutchy. They eat 'em to save fun'ral expenses. I guess this guy went down the wrong way an' they got indigestion.

COCKY Indigestion! Ho yus, not 'arf! Down't yer know as them blokes 'as two stomacks like a bleedin' camel?

DAVIS [*A short, dark man seated on the right of hatch*] An' you seen the two, I s'pect, ain't you?

COCKY [*Scornfully*] Down't be showin' yer igerance be tryin' to make a mock o' me what has seen more o' the world than yeself ever will.

MAX [*A Swedish fireman—from the rear of hatch*] Spin dat yarn, Cocky.

COCKY It's Gawd's troof, what I tole yer. I 'eard it from a bloke what was captured pris'ner by 'em in the Solomon Islands. Shipped wiv 'im one voyage. 'Twas a rare treat to 'ear 'im tell what 'appened to 'im among 'em. [*Musingly*] 'E was a funny bird, 'e was—'ailed from Mile End, 'e did.

DRISCOLL [*With a snort*] Another lyin' Cockney, the loike av yourself!

LAMPS [*A fat Swede who is sitting on a camp stool in front of his door talking with* CHIPS] Where you meet up with him, Cocky?

CHIPS [*A lanky Scotchman—derisively*] In New Guinea, I'll lay my oath!

COCKY [*Defiantly*] Yus! It *was* in New Guinea, time I was shipwrecked there. [*There is a perfect storm of groans and laughter at this speech.*]

YANK [*Getting up*] Yuh know what we said yuh'd get if yuh sprung any of that lyin' New Guinea dope on us again, don't yuh? Close that trap if yuh don't want a duckin' over the side.

COCKY Ow, I was on'y tryin' to edicate yer a bit. [*He sinks into dignified silence.*]

YANK [*Nodding toward the shore*] Don't yuh know this is the West Indies, yuh crazy mut? There ain't no cannibals here. They're only common niggers.

DRISCOLL [*Irritably*] Whativir they are, the divil take their cryin'. It's enough to give a man the jigs listenin' to 'em.

YANK [*With a grin*] What's the matter, Drisc? Yuh're as sore as a boil about somethin'.

DRISCOLL I'm dyin' wid impatience to have a

dhrink; an' that blarsted bumboat naygur woman took her oath she'd bring back rum enough for the lot av us whin she came back on board to-night.

BIG FRANK [*Overhearing this—in a loud eager voice*] You say the bumboat voman vill bring booze?

DRISCOLL [*Sarcastically*] That's right—tell the Old Man about ut, an' the Mate, too. [*All of the crew have edged nearer to* DRISCOLL *and are listening to the conversation with an air of suppressed excitement.* DRISCOLL *lowers his voice impressively and addresses them all.*] She said she cud snake ut on board in the bottoms av thim baskets av fruit they're goin' to bring wid 'em to sell to us for'ard.

THE DONKEYMAN [*An old gray-headed man with a kindly, wrinkled face. He is sitting on a camp stool in front of his door, right front.*] She'll be bringin' some black women with her this time—or times has changed since I put in here last.

DRISCOLL She said she wud—two or three—more, maybe, I dunno. [*This announcement is received with great enthusiasm by all hands.*]

COCKY Wot a bloody lark!

OLSON Py yingo, we have one hell of a time!

DRISCOLL [*Warningly*] Remimber ye must be quiet about ut, ye scuts—wid the dhrink, I mane—ivin if the bosun is ashore. The Old Man ordered her to bring no booze on board or he wudn't buy a thing off av her for the ship.

PADDY [*A squat, ugly Liverpool Irishman*] To the divil wid him!

BIG FRANK [*Turning on him*] Shud up, you

tamn fool, Paddy! You vant make trouble? [*To*
DRISCOLL] You und me, ve keep dem quiet, Drisc.

DRISCOLL   Right ye are, Dutchy. I'll split the
skull av the first wan av ye starts to foight. [*Three
bells are heard striking.*]

DAVIS   Three bells. When's she comin', Drisc?

DRISCOLL   She'll be here any minute now, surely.
[*To* PAUL, *who has returned to his position by the
bulwark after hearing* DRISCOLL'S *news*] D'you see
'em comin', Paul?

PAUL   I don't see anyting like bumboat. [*They
all set themselves to wait, lighting pipes, cigarettes,
and making themselves comfortable. There is a
silence broken only by the mournful singing of the
negroes on shore.*]

SMITTY [*Slowly—with a trace of melancholy*]   I
wish they'd stop that song. It makes you think of—
well—things you ought to forget. Rummy go, what?

COCKY [*Slapping him on the back*]   Cheero, ole
love! We'll be 'avin our rum in arf a mo', Duke.
[*He comes down to the deck, leaving* SMITTY *alone
on the forecastle head.*]

BIG FRANK   Sing someting, Drisc. Den ve don't
hear dot yelling.

DAVIS   Give us a chanty, Drisc.

PADDY   Wan all av us knows.

MAX   We all sing in on chorus.

OLSON   "Rio Grande," Drisc.

BIG FRANK   No, ve don't know dot. Sing "Viskey
Johnny."

CHIPS   "Flyin' Cloud."

COCKY   Now! Guv us "Maid o' Amsterdam."

LAMPS "Santa Anna" iss good one.

DRISCOLL Shut your mouths, all av you. [*Scornfully*] A chanty it ut ye want? I'll bet me whole pay day there's not wan in the crowd 'ceptin' Yank here, an' Ollie, an' meself, an' Lamps an' Cocky, maybe, wud be sailors enough to know the main from the mizzen on a windjammer. Ye've heard the names av chanties but divil a note av the tune or a loine av the words do ye know. There's hardly a rale deepwater sailor lift on the seas, more's the pity.

YANK Give us "Blow The Man Down." We all know some of that. [*A chorus of assenting voices:* Yes!—Righto!—Let 'er drive! Start 'er, Drisc! *etc.*]

DRISCOLL Come in then, all av ye. [*He sings*] As I was a-roamin' down Paradise Street—

ALL Wa-a-ay, blow the man down!

DRISCOLL As I was a-roamin' down Paradise Street—

ALL Give us some time to blow the man down!

CHORUS
Blow the man down, boys, oh, blow
            the man down!
    Wa-a-ay, blow the man down!
    As I was a-roamin' down Paradise
            Street—
        Give us some time to blow the
            man down!

DRISCOLL A pretty young maiden I chanced for to meet.

ALL Wa-a-ay, blow the man down!

DRISCOLL   A pretty young maiden I chanced for to meet.

ALL   Give us some time to blow the man down!

CHORUS
Blow the man down, boys, oh, blow
        the man down!
    Wa-a-ay, blow the man down!
A pretty young maiden I chanced
        for to meet.
    Give us some time to blow the
        man down!

PAUL [*Just as* DRISCOLL *is clearing his throat preparatory to starting the next verse*]   Hay, Driscl! Here she come, I tink. Some bumboat comin' dis way. [*They all rush to the side and look toward the land.*]

YANK   There's five or six of them in it—and they paddle like skirts.

DRISCOLL [*Wildly elated*]   "Hurroo, ye scuts! 'Tis thim right enough. [*He does a few jig steps on the deck.*]

OLSON [*After a pause during which all are watching the approaching boat*]   Py yingo, I see six in boat, yes, sir.

DAVIS   I kin make out the baskets. See 'em there amidships?

BIG FRANK   Vot kind booze dey bring—viskey?

DRISCOLL   Rum, foine West Indy rum wid a kick in ut loike a mule's hoind leg.

LAMPS   Maybe she don't bring any; maybe skipper scare her.

DRISCOLL   Don't be throwin' cold water, Lamps. I'll skin her black hoide off av her if she goes back on her worrd.

YANK   Here they come. Listen to 'em gigglin'. [*Calling*] Oh, you kiddo! [*The sound of women's voices can be heard talking and laughing.*]

DRISCOLL [*Calling*]   Is ut you, Mrs. Old Black Joe?

A WOMAN'S VOICE   'Ullo, Mike! [*There is loud feminine laughter at this retort.*]

DRISCOLL   Shake a leg an' come abord thin.

THE WOMAN'S VOICE   We're a-comin'.

DRISCOLL   Come on, Yank. You an' me'd best be goin' to give 'em a hand wid their truck. 'Twill put 'em in good spirits.

COCKY [*As they start off left*]   Ho, you ain't 'arf a fox, Drisc. Down't drink it all afore we sees it.

DRISCOLL [*Over his shoulder*]   You'll be havin' yours, me sonny bye, don't fret. [*He and* YANK *go off left.*]

COCKY [*Licking his lips*]   Gawd blimey, I can do wiv a wet.

DAVIS   Me, too!

CHIPS   I'll bet there ain't none of us'll let any go to waste.

BIG FRANK   I could trink a whole barrel mineself, py chimminy Christmas!

COCKY   I 'opes all the gels ain't as bloomin' ugly as 'er. Looked like a bloody organ-grinder's monkey, she did. Gawd, I couldn't put up wiv the likes of 'er!

PADDY   Ye'll be lucky if any of thim looks at ye, ye squint-eyed runt.

COCKY [*Angrily*]   Ho, yus? You ain't no bleedin' beauty prize yeself, me man. A 'airy ape, I calls yer.

PADDY [*Walking toward him—truculently*] Whot's thot? Say ut again if ye dare.

COCKY [*His hand on his sheath knife—snarling*] 'Airy ape! That's wot I says! [PADDY *tries to reach him but the others keep them apart.*]

BIG FRANK [*Pushing* PADDY *back*]   Vot's the matter mit you, Paddy. Don't you hear vat Driscoll say —no fighting?

PADDY [*Grumblingly*]   I don't take no back talk from that deck-scrubbin' shrimp.

COCKY   Blarsted coal-puncher! [DRISCOLL *appears wearing a broad grin of satisfaction. The fight is immediately forgotten by the crowd who gather around him with exclamations of eager curiosity:* How is it, Drisc? Any luck? Vot she bring, Drisc? Where's the gels? *etc.*]

DRISCOLL [*With an apprehensive glance back at the bridge*]   Not so loud, for the love av hivin! [*The clamor dies down.*] Yis, she has ut wid her. She'll be here in a minute wid a pint bottle or two for each wan av ye—three shillin's a bottle. So don't be impashunt.

COCKY [*Indignantly*]   Three bob! The bloody cow!

SMITTY [*With an ironic smile*]   Grand larceny, by God! [*They all turn and look up at him, surprised to hear him speak.*]

OLSON Py yingo, we don't pay so much.

BIG FRANK Tamn black tief!

PADDY We'll take ut away from her and give her nothin'.

THE CROWD [*Growling*] Dirty thief! Dot's right! Give her nothin'! Not a bloomin' 'apenny! etc.

DRISCOLL [*Grinning*] Ye can take ut or lave ut, me sonny byes. [*He casts a glance in the direction of the bridge and then reaches inside his shirt and pulls out a pint bottle.*] 'Tis foine rum, the rale stuff. [*He drinks.*] I slipped this wan out av wan av the baskets whin they wasn't lookin'. [*He hands the bottle to* OLSON *who is nearest him.*] Here ye are, Ollie. Take a small sup an' pass ut to the nixt. 'Tisn't much but 'twill serve to take the black taste out av your mouths if ye go aisy wid ut. An' there's buckets more av ut comin'. [*The bottle passes from hand to hand, each man taking a sip and smacking his lips with a deep "Aa-ah" of satisfaction.*]

DAVIS Where's she now, Drisc?

DRISCOLL Up havin' a worrd wid the skipper, makin' arrangements about the money, I s'pose.

DAVIS An' where's the other gels?

DRISCOLL Wid her. There's foive av thim she took aboard—two swate little slips av things, near as white as you an' me are, for that gray-whiskered auld fool, an' the mates—an' the engineers too, maybe. The rist av thim'll be comin' for'ard whin she comes.

COCKY 'E ain't 'arf a funny ole bird, the skipper. Gawd blimey! 'Member when we sailed from 'ome 'ow 'e stands on the bridge lookin' like a bloody ole sky pilot? An' 'is missus dawn on the bloomin' dock 'owlin' fit to kill 'erself? An' 'is kids 'owlin' an' wavin' their 'andkerchiefs? [*With great moral indignation*] An' 'ere 'e is makin' up to a bleedin' nigger! There's a captain for yer! Gawd blimey! Bloody crab, I calls 'im!

DRISCOLL Shut up, ye insect! Sure, it's not you should be talkin', an' you wid a woman an' childer weepin' for ye in iviry divil's port in the wide worrld, if we can believe your own tale av ut.

COCKY [*Still indignant*] I ain't no bloomin' captain, I ain't. I ain't got no missus—reg'lar married, I means. I ain't——

BIG FRANK [*Putting a huge paw over* COCKY'S *mouth*] You ain't going talk so much, you hear? [COCKY *wriggles away from him.*] Say, Drisc, how ve pay dis voman for booze? Ve ain't got no cash.

DRISCOLL It's aisy enough. Each girl'll have a slip av paper wid her an' whin you buy anythin' you write ut down and the price beside ut and sign your name. If ye can't write have some one who can do ut for ye. An' rimimber this: Whin ye buy a bottle av dhrink or [*With a wink*] somethin' else forbid, ye must write down tobaccy or fruit or somethin' the loike av that. Whin she laves the skipper'll pay what's owin' on the paper an' take ut out av your pay. Is ut clear to ye now?

ALL Yes—Clear as day—Aw right, Drisc—Righto—Sure. etc.

DRISCOLL An' don't forgit what I said about bein' quiet wid the dhrink, or the Mate'll be down on our necks an' spile the fun. [*A chorus of assent*]

DAVIS [*Looking aft*] Ain't this them comin'? [*They all look in that direction. The silly laughter of a woman is heard.*]

DRISCOLL Look at Yank, wud ye, wid his arrm around the middle av wan av thim. That lad's not wastin' any toime. [*The four women enter from the left, giggling and whispering to each other. The first three carry baskets on their heads. The youngest and best-looking comes last. YANK has his arm about her waist and is carrying her basket in his other hand. All four are distinct negro types. They wear light-colored, loose-fitting clothes and have bright bandana handkerchiefs on their heads. They put down their baskets on the hatch and sit down beside them. The men crowd around, grinning.*]

BELLA [*She is the oldest, stoutest, and homeliest of the four—grinning back at them*] 'Ullo, boys.

THE OTHER GIRLS 'Ullo, boys.

THE MEN Hello, yourself—Evenin'—Hello—How are you? etc.

BELLA [*Genially*] Hope you had a nice voyage. My name's Bella, this here's Susie, yander's Violet, and her there [*Pointing to the girl with YANK*] is Pearl. Now we all knows each other.

PADDY [*Roughly*] Never mind the girls. Where's the dhrink?

BELLA [*Tartly*] You're a hawg, ain't you? Don't talk so loud or you don't git any—you nor no man. Think I wants the ole captain to put me off the ship, do you?"

YANK Yes, nix on hollerin', you! D'yuh wanta queer all of us?

BELLA [*Casting a quick glance over her shoulder*] Here! Some of you big strapping boys sit back of us on the hatch there so's them officers can't see what we're doin'. [DRISCOLL *and several of the others sit and stand in back of the girls on the hatch.* BELLA *turns to* DRISCOLL.] Did you tell 'em they gotter sign for what they gits—and *how* to sign?

DRISCOLL I did—what's your name again—oh, yis —Bella, darlin'.

BELLA Then it's all right; but you boys has gotter go inside the fo'castle when you gits your bottle. No drinkin' out here on deck. I ain't takin' no chances. [*An impatient murmur of assent goes up from the crowd.*] Ain't that right, Mike?

DRISCOLL Right as rain, darlin'. [BIG FRANK *leans over and says something to him in a low voice.* DRISCOLL *laughs and slaps his thigh.*] Listen, Bella, I've somethin' to ask ye for my little friend here who's bashful. Ut has to do wid the ladies so I'd best be whisperin' ut to ye meself to kape them from blushin'. [*He leans over and asks her a question.*]

BELLA [*Firmly*] Four shillin's.

DRISCOLL [*Laughing*] D'you hear that, all av ye? Four shillin's ut is.

PADDY [*Angrily*] To hell wid this talkin'. I want a dhrink.

BELLA Is everything all right, Mike?

DRISCOLL [*After a look back at the bridge*] Sure. Let her droive!

BELLA All right, girls. [*The girls reach down in their baskets in under the fruit which is on top and each pulls out a pint bottle. Four of the men crowd up and take the bottles.*] Fetch a light, Lamps, that's a good boy. [LAMPS *goes to his room and returns with a candle. This is passed from one girl to another as the men sign the sheets of paper for their bottles.*] Don't you boys forget to mark down cigarettes or tobacco or fruit, remember! Three shillin's is the price. Take it into the fo'castle. For Gawd's sake, don't stand out here drinkin' in the moonlight. [*The four go into the forecastle. Four more take their places.* PADDY *plants himself in front of* PEARL *who is sitting by* YANK *with his arm still around her.*]

PADDY [*Gruffly*]   Gimme thot! [*She holds out a bottle which he snatches from her hand. He turns to go away.*]

YANK [*Sharply*]   Here, you! Where d'yuh get that stuff? You ain't signed for that yet.

PADDY [*Sullenly*]   I can't write me name.

YANK   Then I'll write it for yuh. [*He takes the paper from* PEARL *and writes.*] There ain't goin' to be no welchin' on little Bright Eyes here—not when I'm around, see? Ain't I right, kiddo?

PEARL [*With a grin*]   Yes, suh.

BELLA [*Seeing all four are served*]   Take it into the fo'castle, boys. [PADDY *defiantly raises his bottle and gulps down a drink in the full moonlight.* BELLA *sees him.*] Look at 'im! Look at the dirty swine! [PADDY *slouches into the forecastle.*] Wants to git me in trouble. That settles it! We all got to git inside, boys, where we won't git caught. Come on, girls. [*The girls pick up their baskets and follow*

BELLA. YANK *and* PEARL *are the last to reach the doorway. She lingers behind him, her eyes fixed on* SMITTY, *who is still sitting on the forecastle head, his chin on his hands, staring off into vacancy.*]

PEARL [*Waving a hand to attract his attention*] Come ahn in, pretty boy. Ah likes you.

SMITTY [*Coldly*] Yes; I want to buy a bottle, please. [*He goes down the steps and follows her into the forecastle. No one remains on deck but the* DONKEYMAN, *who sits smoking his pipe in front of his door. There is the subdued babble of voices from the crowd inside but the mournful cadence of the song from the shore can again be faintly heard.* SMITTY *reappears and closes the door to the forecastle after him. He shudders and shakes his shoulders as if flinging off something which disgusted him. Then he lifts the bottle which is in his hand to his lips and gulps down a long drink.* THE DONKEYMAN *watches him impassively.* SMITTY *sits down on the hatch facing him. Now that the closed door has shut off nearly all the noise the singing from shore comes clearly over the moonlit water.*]

SMITTY [*Listening to it for a moment*] Damn that song of theirs. [*He takes another big drink.*] What do you say, Donk?

THE DONKEYMAN [*Quietly*] Seems nice an' sleepy-like.

SMITTY [*With a hard laugh*] Sleepy! If I listened to it long—sober—I'd never go to sleep.

THE DONKEYMAN 'Tain't sich bad music, is it? Sounds kinder pretty to me—low an' mournful—

same as listenin' to the organ outside o' church of a Sunday.

SMITTY [*With a touch of impatience*] I didn't mean it was bad music. It isn't. It's the beastly memories the damn thing brings up—for some reason. [*He takes another pull at the bottle.*]

THE DONKEYMAN Ever hear it before?

SMITTY No; never in my life. It's just a something about the rotten thing which makes me think of—well—oh, the devil! [*He forces a laugh.*]

THE DONKEYMAN [*Spitting placidly*] Queer things, mem'ries. I ain't ever been bothered much by 'em.

SMITTY [*Looking at him fixedly for a moment— with quiet scorn*] No, you wouldn't be.

THE DONKEYMAN Not that I ain't had my share o' things goin' wrong; but I puts 'em out o' me mind, like, an' fergets 'em.

SMITTY But suppose you couldn't put them out of your mind? Suppose they haunted you when you were awake and when you were asleep—what then?

THE DONKEYMAN [*Quietly*] I'd git drunk, same's you're doin'.

SMITTY [*With a harsh laugh*] Good advice. [*He takes another drink. He is beginning to show the effects of the liquor. His face is flushed and he talks rather wildly.*] We're poor little lambs who have lost our way, eh, Donk? Damned from here to eternity, what? God have mercy on such as we! True, isn't it, Donk?

THE DONKEYMAN Maybe; I dunno. [*After a*

slight pause] Whatever set you goin' to sea? You ain't made for it.

SMITTY [*Laughing wildly*]   My old friend in the bottle here, Donk.

THE DONKEYMAN   I done my share o' drinkin' in my time. [*Regretfully*] Them was good times, those days. Can't hold up under drink no more. Doctor told me I'd got to stop or die. [*He spits contentedly.*] So I stops.

SMITTY [*With a foolish smile*]   Then I'll drink one for you. Here's your health, old top! [*He drinks.*]

THE DONKEYMAN [*After a pause*]   S'pose there's a gel mixed up in it someplace, ain't there?

SMITTY [*Stiffly*]   What makes you think so?

THE DONKEYMAN   Always is when a man lets music bother 'im. [*After a few puffs at his pipe*] An' she said she threw you over 'cause you was drunk; an' you said you was drunk 'cause she threw you over. [*He spits leisurely.*] Queer thing, love, ain't it?

SMITTY [*Rising to his feet with drunken dignity*]. I'll trouble you not to pry into my affairs, Donkeyman.

THE DONKEYMAN [*Unmoved*]   That's everybody's affair, what I said. I been through it many's the time. [*Genially*] I always hit 'em a whack on the ear an' went out and got drunker'n ever. When I come home again they always had somethin' special nice cooked fur me to eat. [*Puffing at his pipe*] That's the on'y way to fix 'em when they gits on their high horse. I don't s'pose you ever tried that?

SMITTY [*Pompously*] Gentlemen don't hit women.

THE DONKEYMAN [*Placidly*] No; that's why they has mem'ries when they hears music. [SMITTY *does not deign to reply to this but sinks into a scornful silence.* DAVIS *and the girl* VIOLET *come out of the forecastle and close the door behind them. He is staggering a bit and she is laughing shrilly.*]

DAVIS [*Turning to the left*] This way, Rose, or Pansy, or Jessamine, or black Tulip, or Violet, or whatever the hell flower your name is. No one'll see us back here. [*They go off left.*]

THE DONKEYMAN There's love at first sight for you—an' plenty more o' the same in the fo'c's'tle. No mem'ries jined with that.

SMITTY [*Really repelled*] Shut up, Donk. You're disgusting. [*He takes a long drink.*]

THE DONKEYMAN [*Philosophically*] All depends on how you was brung up, I s'pose. [PEARL *comes out of the forecastle. There is a roar of voices from inside. She shuts the door behind her, sees* SMITTY *on the hatch, and comes over and sits beside him and puts her arm over his shoulder.*]

THE DONKEYMAN [*Chuckling*] There's love for you, Duke.

PEARL [*Patting* SMITTY's *face with her hand*] 'Ullo, pretty boy. [SMITTY *pushes her hand away coldly.*] What you doin' out here all alone by yourself?

SMITTY [*With a twisted grin*] Thinking and— [*He indicates the bottle in his hand*]—drinking to stop thinking. [*He drinks and laughs maudlinly. The bottle is three-quarters empty.*]

PEARL You oughtn't drink so much, pretty boy. Don' you know dat? You have big, big headache come mawnin'.

SMITTY [*Dryly*] Indeed?

PEARL Tha's true. Ah knows what Ah say. [*Cooingly*] Why you run 'way from me, pretty boy? Ah likes you. Ah don' like them other fellahs. They act too rough. You ain't rough. You're a genelman. Ah knows. Ah can tell a genelman fahs Ah can see 'im.

SMITTY Thank you for the compliment; but you're wrong, you see. I'm merely—a ranker. [*He adds bitterly*] And a rotter.

PEARL [*Patting his arm*] No, you ain't. Ah knows better. You're a genelman. [*Insinuatingly*] Ah wouldn't have nothin' to do with them other men, but [*She smiles at him enticingly*] you is diff'rent. [*He pushes her away from him disgustedly. She pouts.*] Don' you like me, pretty boy?

SMITTY [*A bit ashamed*] I beg your pardon. I didn't mean to be rude, you know, really. [*His politeness is drunkenly exaggerated.*] I'm a bit off color.

PEARL [*Brightening up*] Den you do like me—little ways?

SMITTY [*Carelessly*] Yes, yes, why shouldn't I? [*He suddenly laughs wildly and puts his arm around her waist and presses her to him.*] Why not? [*He pulls his arm back quickly with a shudder of disgust, and takes a drink. PEARL looks at him curiously, puzzled by his strange actions. The door from*

the forecastle is kicked open and YANK *comes out.
The uproar of shouting, laughing and singing
voices has increased in violence.* YANK *staggers over
toward* SMITTY *and* PEARL.]

YANK [*Blinking at them*]   What the hell—oh, it's
you, Smitty the Duke. I was goin' to turn one loose
on the jaw of any guy'd cop my dame, but seein' it's
you—— [*Sentimentally*] Pals is pals and any pal of
mine c'n have anythin' I got, see? [*Holding out his
hand*] Shake, Duke. [SMITTY *takes his hand and he
pumps it up and down.*] You'n me's frens. Ain't I
right?

SMITTY   Right it is, Yank. But you're wrong
about this girl. She isn't with me. She was just going
back to the fo'c's'tle to you. [PEARL *looks at him
with hatred gathering in her eyes.*]

YANK   Tha' right?

SMITTY   On my word!

YANK [*Grabbing her arm*]   Come on then, you,
Pearl! Le's have a drink with the bunch. [*He pulls
her to the entrance, where she shakes off his hand
long enough to turn on* SMITTY *furiously.*]

PEARL   You swine! You can go to hell! [*She goes
in the forecastle, slamming the door.*]

THE DONKEYMAN [*Spitting calmly*]   There's love
for you. They're all the same—white, brown, yeller
'n' black. A whack on the ear's the only thing'll
learn 'em. [SMITTY *makes no reply but laughs
harshly and takes another drink; then sits staring
before him, the almost empty bottle tightly clutched
in one hand. There is an increase in volume of the
muffled clamor from the forecastle and a moment*

*later the door is thrown open and the whole mob,
led by* DRISCOLL, *pours out on deck. All of them are
very drunk and several of them carry bottles in their
hands.* BELLA *is the only one of the women who is
absolutely sober. She tries in vain to keep the men
quiet.* PEARL *drinks from* YANK'S *bottle every moment or so, laughing shrilly, and leaning against*
YANK, *whose arm is about her waist.* PAUL *comes
out last carrying an accordion. He staggers over and
stands on top of the hatch, his instrument under his
arm.*]

DRISCOLL   Play us a dance, ye square-head swab!
—a rale, Godforsaken son av a turkey trot wid guts
to ut.

YANK   Straight from the old Barbary Coast in
Frisco!

PAUL   I don' know. I try. [*He commences tuning
up.*]

YANK   Ataboy! Let 'er rip! [DAVIS *and* VIOLET
come back and join the crowd. THE DONKEYMAN
looks on them all with a detached, indulgent air.
SMITTY *stares before him and does not seem to know
there is any one on deck but himself.*]

BIG FRANK   Dance? I don't dance. I trink! [*He
suits the action to the word and roars with mean-
ingless laughter.*]

DRISCOLL   Git out av the way thin, ye big hulk,
an' give us some room. [BIG FRANK *sits down on the
hatch, right. All of the others who are not going to
dance either follow his example or lean against the
port bulwark.*]

BELLA [*On the verge of tears at her inability to*

*keep them in the forecastle or make them be quiet
now they are out]* For Gawd's sake, boys, don't
shout so loud! Want to git me in trouble?

DRISCOLL [*Grabbing her*] Dance wid me, me
cannibal quane. [*Some one drops a bottle on deck
and it smashes.*]

BELLA [*Hysterically*] There they goes! There
they goes! Captain'll hear that! Oh, my Lawd!

DRISCOLL Be damned to him! Here's the music!
Off ye go! [PAUL *starts playing "You Great Big
Beautiful Doll" with a note left out every now and
then. The four couples commence dancing—a jerk-
shouldered version of the old Turkey Trot as it was
done in the sailor-town dives, made more grotesque
by the fact that all the couples are drunk and keep
lurching into each other every moment. Two of the
men start dancing together, intentionally bumping
into the others. *YANK *and *PEARL *come around in
front of *SMITTY *and, as they pass him, *PEARL *slaps
him across the side of the face with all her might,
and laughs viciously. He jumps to his feet with his
fists clenched but sees who hit him and sits down
again smiling bitterly. *YANK *laughs boisterously.*]

YANK Wow! Some wallop! One on you, Duke.

DRISCOLL [*Hurling his cap at* PAUL] Faster, ye
toad! [PAUL *makes frantic efforts to speed up and
the music suffers in the process.*]

BELLA [*Puffing*] Let me go. I'm wore out with
you steppin' on my toes, you clumsy Mick. [*She
struggles but* DRISCOLL *holds her tight.*]

DRISCOLL God blarst you for havin' such big
feet, thin. Aisy, aisy, Mrs. Old Black Joe! 'Tis

dancin'll take the blubber off ye. [*He whirls her around the deck by main force.* COCKY, *with* SUSIE, *is dancing near the hatch, right, when* PADDY, *who is sitting on the edge with* BIG FRANK, *sticks his foot out and the wavering couple stumble over it and fall flat on the deck. A roar of laughter goes up.* COCKY *rises to his feet, his face livid with rage, and springs at* PADDY, *who promptly knocks him down.* DRISCOLL *hits* PADDY *and* BIG FRANK *hits* DRISCOLL. *In a flash a wholesale fight has broken out and the deck is a surging crowd of drink-maddened men hitting out at each other indiscriminately, although the general idea seems to be a battle between seamen and firemen. The women shriek and take refuge on top of the hatch, where they huddle in a frightened group. Finally there is the flash of a knife held high in the moonlight and a loud yell of pain.*]

DAVIS [*Somewhere in the crowd*] Here's the Mate comin'! Let's git out o' this! [*There is a general rush for the forecastle. In a moment there is no one left on deck but the little group of women on the hatch;* SMITTY, *still dazedly rubbing his cheek;* THE DONKEYMAN *quietly smoking on his stool; and* YANK *and* DRISCOLL, *their faces battered up considerably, their undershirts in shreds, bending over the still form of* PADDY, *which lies stretched out on the deck between them. In the silence the mournful chant from the shore creeps slowly out to the ship.*]

DRISCOLL [*Quickly—in a low voice*] Who knoifed him?

YANK [*Stupidly*] I didn't see it. How do I know?

COCKY, I'll bet. [*The* FIRST MATE *enters from the left. He is a tall, strongly-built man dressed in a plain blue uniform.*]

THE MATE [*Angrily*] What's all this noise about? [*He sees the man lying on the deck.*] Hello! What's this? [*He bends down on one knee beside* PADDY.]

DRISCOLL [*Stammering*] All av us—was in a bit av a harmless foight, sir—an'—I dunno—— [THE MATE *rolls* PADDY *over and sees a knife wound on his shoulder.*]

THE MATE Knifed, by God. [*He takes an electric flash from his pocket and examines the cut.*] Lucky it's only a flesh wound. He must have hit his head on deck when he fell. That's what knocked him out. This is only a scratch. Take him aft and I'll bandage him up.

DRISCOLL Yis, sor. [*They take* PADDY *by the shoulders and feet and carry him off left. The* MATE *looks up and sees the women on the hatch for the first time.*]

THE MATE [*Surprised*] Hello! [*He walks over to them.*] Go to the cabin and get your money and clear off. If I had my way, you'd never—— [*His foot hits a bottle. He stoops down and picks it up and smells of it.*] Rum, by God! So that's the trouble! I thought their breaths smelled damn queer. [*To the women, harshly*] You needn't go to the skipper for any money. You won't get any. That'll teach you to smuggle rum on a ship and start a riot.

BELLA But, Mister——

THE MATE [*Sternly*] You know the agreement—rum—no money.

BELLA [*Indignantly*] Honest to Gawd, Mister, I never brung no——

THE MATE [*Fiercely*] You're a liar! And none of your lip or I'll make a complaint ashore tomorrow and have you locked up.

BELLA [*Subdued*] Please, Mister——

THE MATE Clear out of this, now! Not another word out of you! Tumble over the side damn quick! The two others are waiting for you. Hop, now! [*They walk quickly—almost run—off to the left.* THE MATE *follows them, nodding to* THE DONKEY-MAN, *and ignoring the oblivious* SMITTY.]

[*There is absolute silence on the ship for a few moments. The melancholy song of the negroes drifts crooning over the water.* SMITTY *listens to it intently for a time; then sighs heavily, a sigh that is half a sob.*]

SMITTY God! [*He drinks the last drop in the bottle and throws it behind him on the hatch.*]

THE DONKEYMAN [*Spitting tranquilly*] More mem'ries? [SMITTY *does not answer him. The ship's bell tolls four bells.* THE DONKEYMAN *knocks out his pipe.*] I think I'll turn in. [*He opens the door to his cabin, but turns to look at* SMITTY—*kindly.*] You can't hear it in the fo'c's'le—the music, I mean—an' there'll likely be more drink in there, too. Good night. [*He goes in and shuts the door.*]

SMITTY Good night, Donk. [*He gets wearily to his feet and walks with bowed shoulders, staggering a bit, to the forecastle entrance and goes in. There is silence for a second or so, broken only by the haunted, saddened voice of that brooding music, faint and far-off, like the mood of the moonlight made audible.*]

[*The curtain falls.*]

BOUND EAST
FOR CARDIFF

A Play in One Act

CHARACTERS

Yank
Driscoll
Cocky
Davis
Scotty
Olson
Paul
Smitty
Ivan
The Captain
The Second Mate

BOUND EAST
FOR CARDIFF

SCENE *The seamen's forecastle of the British tramp steamer* Glencairn *on a foggy night midway on the voyage between New York and Cardiff. An irregularly shaped compartment, the sides of which almost meet at the far end to form a triangle. Sleeping bunks about six feet long, ranged three deep with a space of three feet separating the upper from the lower, are built against the sides. On the right above the bunks three or four portholes can be seen. In front of the bunks, rough wooden benches. Over the bunks on the left, a lamp in a bracket. In the left foreground, a doorway. On the floor near it, a pail with a tin dipper. Oilskins are hanging from a hook near the doorway.*

The far side of the forecastle is so narrow that it contains only one series of bunks.

In under the bunks a glimpse can be had of seachests, suit cases, seaboots, etc., jammed in indiscriminately.

At regular intervals of a minute or so the blast of the steamer's whistle can be heard above all the other sounds.

Five men are sitting on the benches talking. They are dressed in dirty patched suits of dungaree, flannel shirts, and all are in their stocking feet. Four of the men are pulling on pipes and the air is heavy with rancid tobacco smoke. Sitting on the top bunk in the left foreground, a Norwegian, Paul, is softly playing some folk song on a battered accordion. He stops from time to time to listen to the conversation.

In the lower bunk in the rear a dark-haired, hard-featured man is lying apparently asleep. One of his arms is stretched limply over the side of the bunk. His face is very pale, and drops of clammy perspiration glisten on his forehead.

It is nearing the end of the dog watch— about ten minutes to eight in the evening.

COCKY [*A weazened runt of a man. He is telling a story. The others are listening with amused, incredulous faces, interrupting him at the end of each sentence with loud derisive guffaws.*] Makin' love to me, she was! It's Gawd's truth! A bloomin' nigger! Greased all over with cocoanut oil, she was. Gawd blimey, I couldn't stand 'er. Bloody old cow, I says; and with that I fetched 'er a biff on the ear wot knocked 'er silly, an'—— [*He is interrupted by a roar of laughter from the others.*]

DAVIS [*A middle-aged man with black hair and mustache*]   You're a liar, Cocky.

SCOTTY [*A dark young fellow*]   Ho-ho! Ye werr neverr in New Guinea in yourr life, I'm thinkin'.

OLSON [*A Swede with a drooping blond mustache —with ponderous sarcasm*]   Yust tink of it! You say she wass a cannibal, Cocky?

DRISCOLL [*A brawny Irishman with the battered features of a prizefighter*]   How cud ye doubt ut, Ollie? A quane av the naygurs she musta been surely. Who else wud think herself aqual to fallin' in love wid a beauthiful, divil-may-care rake av a man the loike av Cocky? [*A burst of laughter from the crowd*]

COCKY [*Indignantly*]   Gawd strike me dead if it ain't true, every bleedin' word of it. 'Appened ten year ago come Christmas.

SCOTTY   'Twas a Christmas dinner she had her eyes on.

DAVIS   He'd a been a tough old bird.

DRISCOLL   'Tis lucky for both av ye ye escaped; for the quane av the cannibal isles wad 'a died av the belly ache the day afther Christmas, divil a doubt av ut. [*The laughter at this is long and loud.*]

COCKY [*Sullenly*]   Blarsted fat 'eads! [*The sick man in the lower bunk in the rear groans and moves restlessly. There is a hushed silence. All the men turn and stare at him.*]

DRISCOLL   Ssshh! [*In a hushed whisper*]   We'd best not be talkin' so loud and him tryin' to have a bit av a sleep. [*He tiptoes softly to the side of the bunk.*] Yank! You'd be wantin' a drink av wather, maybe? [YANK *does not reply.* DRISCOLL *bends over and looks at him.*] It's asleep he is, sure enough. His breath is chokin' in his throat loike wather gurglin' in a poipe. [*He comes back quietly and sits down. All are silent, avoiding each other's eyes.*]

COCKY [*After a pause*] Pore devil! It's over the side for 'im, Gawd 'elp 'im.

DRISCOLL Stop your croakin'! He's not dead yet and, praise God, he'll have many a long day yet before him.

SCOTTY [*Shaking his head doubtfully*] He's bod, mon, he's verry bod.

DAVIS Lucky he's alive. Many a man's light woulda gone out after a fall like that.

OLSON You saw him fall?

DAVIS Right next to him. He and me was goin' down in number two hold to do some chippin'. He puts his leg over careless-like and misses the ladder and plumps straight down to the bottom. I was scared to look over for a minute, and then I heard him groan and I scuttled down after him. He was hurt bad inside for the blood was drippin' from the side of his mouth. He was groanin' hard, but he never let a word out of him.

COCKY An' you blokes remember when we 'auled 'im in 'ere? Oh, 'ell, 'e says, oh, 'ell—like that, and nothink else.

OLSON Did the captain know where he iss hurted?

COCKY That silly ol' josser! Wot the 'ell would 'e know abaht anythink?

SCOTTY [*Scornfully*]   He fiddles in his mouth wi'
a bit of glass.

DRISCOLL [*Angrily*]   The divil's own life ut is to
be out on the lonely sea wid nothin' betune you
and a grave in the ocean but a spindle-shanked,
gray-whiskered auld fool the loike av him. 'Twas
enough to make a saint shwear to see him wid his
gold watch in his hand, tryin' to look as wise as an
owl on a tree, and all the toime he not knowin'
whether 'twas cholery or the barber's itch was the
matther wid Yank.

SCOTTY [*Sardonically*]   He gave him a dose of
salts, na doot?

DRISCOLL   Divil a thing he gave him at all, but
looked in the book he had wid him, and shook his
head, and walked out widout sayin' a word, the
second mate afther him no wiser than himself,
God's curse on the two av thim!

COCKY [*After a pause*]   Yank was a good shipmate, pore beggar. Lend me four bob in Noo Yark,
'e did.

DRISCOLL [*Warmly*]   A good shipmate he was
and is, none betther. Ye said no more than the
truth, Cocky. Five years and more ut is since first
I shipped wid him, and we've stuck together iver
since through good luck and bad. Fights we've had,
God help us, but 'twas only when we'd a bit av
drink taken, and we always shook hands the nixt
mornin'. Whativer was his was mine, and many's
the toime I'd a been on the beach or worse, but
for him. And now—— [*His voice trembles as he*

fights to control his emotion.] Divil take me if I'm not startin' to blubber loike an auld woman, and he not dead at all, but goin' to live many a long year yet, maybe.

DAVIS   The sleep'll do him good. He seems better now.

OLSON   If he wude eat someting——

DRISCOLL   Wud ye have him be eatin' in his condishun? Sure it's hard enough on the rest av us wid nothin' the matther wid our insides to be stomachin' the skoff on this rusty lime-juicer.

SCOTTY [*Indignantly*]   It's a starvation ship.

DAVIS   Plenty o' work and no food—and the owners ridin' around in carriages!

OLSON   Hash, hash! Stew, stew! Marmalade, py damn! [*He spits disgustedly.*]

COCKY   Bloody swill! Fit only for swine is wot I say.

DRISCOLL   And the dishwather they disguise wid the name av tea! And the putty they call bread! My belly feels loike I'd swalleyed a dozen rivets at the thought av ut! And sea-biscuit that'd break the teeth av a lion if he had the misfortune to take a bite at one! [*Unconsciously they have all raised their voices, forgetting the sick man in their sailor's delight at finding something to grumble about.*]

PAUL [*Swings his feet over the side of his bunk, stops playing his accordion, and says slowly*]   And rot-ten po-tay-toes! [*He starts in playing again. The sick man gives a groan of pain.*]

DRISCOLL [*Holding up his hand*]   Shut your mouths, all av you. 'Tis a hell av a thing for us to be complainin' about our guts, and a sick man maybe dyin' listenin' to us. [*Gets up and shakes his fist at the Norwegian.*] God stiffen you, ye squarehead scut! Put down that organ av yours or I'll break your ugly face for you. Is that banshee schreechin' fit music for a sick man? [*The Norwegian puts his accordion in the bunk and lies back and closes his eyes.* DRISCOLL *goes over and stands beside* YANK. *The steamer's whistle sounds particularly loud in the silence.*]

DAVIS   Damn this fog! [*Reaches in under a bunk and yanks out a pair of seaboots, which he pulls on.*] My lookout next, too. Must be nearly eight bells, boys. [*With the exception of* OLSON, *all the men sitting up put on oilskins, sou'westers, seaboots, etc., in preparation for the watch on deck.* OLSON *crawls into a lower bunk on the right.*]

SCOTTY   My wheel.

OLSON   [*Disgustedly*] Nothin' but yust dirty weather all dis voyage. I yust can't sleep when weestle blow. [*He turns his back to the light and is soon fast asleep and snoring.*]

SCOTTY   If this fog keeps up, I'm tellin' ye, we'll no be in Carrdiff for a week or more.

DRISCOLL   'Twas just such a night as this the auld Dover wint down. Just about this toime ut was, too, and we all sittin' round in the fo'castle, Yank beside me, whin all av a suddint we heard a great slitherin' crash, and the ship heeled over till we was all in a heap on wan side. What came afther I disremimber exactly, except 'twas a hard shift to get the boats over the side before the auld teakittle sank. Yank was in the same boat wid me, and sivin morthal days we drifted wid scarcely a drop of wather or a bite to chew on. 'Twas Yank here that held me down whin I wanted to jump into the ocean, roarin' mad wid the thirst. Picked up we were on the same day wid only Yank in his senses, and him steerin' the boat.

COCKY [*Protestingly*]   Blimey but you're a cheerful blighter, Driscoll! Talkin' abaht shipwrecks in this 'ere blushin' fog. [YANK *groans and stirs uneasily, opening his eyes.* DRISCOLL *hurries to his side.*]

DRISCOLL   Are ye feelin' any betther, Yank?

YANK [*In a weak voice*]   No.

DRISCOLL   Sure, you must be. You look as sthrong as an ox. [*Appealing to the others*] Am I tellin' him a lie?

DAVIS   The sleep's done you good.

COCKY   You'll be 'avin your pint of beer in Cardiff this day week.

SCOTTY   And fish and chips, mon!

YANK [*Peevishly*]   What're yuh all lyin' fur? D'yuh think I'm scared to—— [*He hesitates as if frightened by the word he is about to say.*]

DRISCOLL   Don't be thinkin' such things! [*The ship's bell is heard heavily tolling eight times. From the forecastle head above the voice of the lookout rises in a long wail:* Aaall's welll. *The men look uncertainly at* YANK *as if undecided whether to say good-bye or not.*]

YANK [*In an agony of fear*]   Don't leave me, Driscl! I'm dyin', I tell yuh. I won't stay here alone with every one snorin'. I'll go out on deck. [*He makes a feeble attempt to rise, but sinks back with a sharp groan. His breath comes in wheezy gasps.*] Don't leave me, Drisc! [*His face grows white and his head falls back with a jerk.*]

DRISCOLL   Don't be worryin', Yank. I'll not move a step out av here—and let that divil av a bosun curse his black head off. You speak a word to the bosun, Cocky. Tell him that Yank is bad took and I'll be stayin' wid him a while yet.

COCKY   Right-o. [COCKY, DAVIS, *and* SCOTTY *go out quietly.*]

COCKY [*From the alleyway*]   Gawd blimey, the fog's thick as soup.

DRISCOLL   Are ye satisfied now, Yank? [*Receiving no answer, he bends over the still form.*] He's fainted, God help him! [*He gets a tin dipper from the bucket and bathes* YANK'S *forehead with the water.* YANK *shudders and opens his eyes.*]

YANK [*Slowly*]   I thought I was goin' then. Wha' did yuh wanta wake me up fur?

DRISCOLL [*With forced gayety*]   Is it wishful for heaven ye are?

YANK [*Gloomily*]   Hell, I guess.

DRISCOLL [*Crossing himself involuntarily*]   For the love av the saints don't be talkin' loike that! You'd give a man the creeps. It's chippin' rust on deck you'll be in a day or two wid the best av us. [YANK *does not answer, but closes his eyes wearily. The seaman who has been on lookout,* SMITTY, *a young Englishman, comes in and takes off his dripping oilskins. While he is doing this the man whose*

*turn at the wheel has been relieved enters. He is
a dark burly fellow with a round stupid face. The
Englishman steps softly over to* DRISCOLL. *The
other crawls into a lower bunk.*]

SMITTY [*Whispering*]   How's Yank?

DRISCOLL   Betther. Ask him yourself. He's
awake.

YANK   I'm all right, Smitty.

SMITTY   Glad to hear it, Yank. [*He crawls to
an upper bunk and is soon asleep.*]

IVAN [*The stupid-faced seaman who came in after* SMITTY *twists his head in the direction of the
sick man.*]   You feel gude, Jank?

YANK [*Wearily*]   Yes, Ivan.

IVAN   Dot's gude. [*He rolls over on his side and
falls asleep immediately.*]

YANK [*After a pause broken only by snores—with
a bitter laugh*]   Good-by and good luck to the lot
of you!

DRISCOLL   Is ut painin' you again?

YANK   It hurts like hell—here. [*He points to
the lower part of his chest on the left side.*] I guess
my old pump's busted. Ooohh! [*A spasm of pain
contracts his pale features. He presses his hand to
his side and writhes on the thin mattress of his bunk.
The perspiration stands out in beads on his forehead.*]

DRISCOLL [*Terrified*]   Yank! Yank! What is ut?
[*Jumping to his feet*] I'll run for the captain. [*He
starts for the doorway.*]

YANK [*Sitting up in his bunk, frantic with fear*]

Don't leave me, Drisc! For God's sake, don't leave me alone! [*He leans over the side of his bunk and spits.* DRISCOLL *comes back to him.*] Blood! Ugh!

DRISCOLL   Blood again! I'd best be gettin' the captain.

YANK   No, no, don't leave me! If yuh do I'll git up and follow you. I ain't no coward, but I'm scared to stay here with all of them asleep and snorin.' [DRISCOLL, *not knowing what to do, sits down on the bench beside him. He grows calmer and sinks back on the mattress.*] The captain can't do me no good, yuh know it yourself. The pain ain't so bad now, but I thought it had me then. It was like a buzz-saw cuttin' into me.

DRISCOLL [*Fiercely*]   God blarst ut!

[*The* CAPTAIN *and the* SECOND MATE *of the steamer enter the forecastle. The* CAPTAIN *is an old man with gray mustache and whiskers. The* MATE *is clean-shaven and middle-aged. Both are dressed in simple blue uniforms.*]

THE CAPTAIN [*Taking out his watch and feeling* YANK's *pulse*]   And how is the sick man?

YANK [*Feebly*]   All right, sir.

THE CAPTAIN   And the pain in the chest?

YANK   It still hurts, sir, worse than ever.

THE CAPTAIN [*Taking a thermometer from his pocket and putting it into* YANK's *mouth*]   Here. Be sure and keep this in under your tongue, not over it.

THE MATE [*After a pause*]   Isn't this your watch on deck, DRISCOLL?

DRISCOLL   Yes, sorr, but Yank was fearin' to be alone, and—

THE CAPTAIN   That's all right, Driscoll.

DRISCOLL   Thank ye, sorr.

THE CAPTAIN [*Stares at his watch for a moment or so; then takes the thermometer from* YANK'S *mouth and goes to the lamp to read it. His expression grows very grave. He beckons the* MATE *and* DRISCOLL *to the corner near the doorway.* YANK *watches them furtively. The* CAPTAIN *speaks in a low voice to the* MATE] Way up, both of them. [*To* DRISCOLL] Has he been spitting blood again?

DRISCOLL   Not much for the hour just past, sorr, but before that—

THE CAPTAIN   A great deal?

DRISCOLL   Yes, sorr.

THE CAPTAIN   He hasn't eaten anything?

DRISCOLL   No, sorr.

THE CAPTAIN   Did he drink that medicine I sent him?

DRISCOLL   Yes, sorr, but it didn't stay down.

THE CAPTAIN [*Shaking his head*] I'm afraid—he's very weak. I can't do anything else for him. It's too serious for me. If this had only happened a week later we'd be in Cardiff in time to——

DRISCOLL   Plaze help him some way, sorr!

THE CAPTAIN [*Impatiently*] But, my good man, I'm not a doctor. [*More kindly as he sees* DRISCOLL'S *grief*] You and he have been shipmates a long time?

DRISCOLL   Five years and more, sorr.

THE CAPTAIN   I see. Well, don't let him move.

Keep him quiet and we'll hope for the best. I'll read the matter up and send him some medicine, something to ease the pain, anyway. [*Goes over to* YANK.] Keep up your courage! You'll be better to morrow. [*He breaks down lamely before* YANK's *steady gaze.*] We'll pull you through all right—and—hm—well—coming, Robinson? Dammit! [*He goes out hurriedly, followed by the* MATE.]

DRISCOLL [*Trying to conceal his anxiety*]   Didn't I tell you you wasn't half as sick as you thought you was? The Captain'll have you out on deck cursin' and swearin' loike a trooper before the week is out.

YANK   Don't lie, Drisc. I heard what he said, and if I didn't I c'd tell by the way I feel. I know what's goin' to happen. I'm goin' to—— [*He hesitates for a second—then resolutely*] I'm goin' to die, that's what, and the sooner the better!

DRISCOLL [*Wildly*]   No, and be damned to you, you're not. I'll not let you.

YANK   It ain't no use, Drisc. I ain't got a chance, but I ain't scared. Gimme a drink of water, will yuh, Drisc? My throat's burnin' up. [DRISCOLL *brings the dipper full of water and supports his head while he drinks in great gulps.*]

DRISCOLL [*Seeking vainly for some word of comfort*]   Are ye feelin' more aisy loike now?

YANK   Yes—now—when I know it's all up. [*A pause*] You mustn't take it so hard, Drisc. I was just thinkin' it ain't as bad as people think—dyin'. I ain't never took much stock in the truck them sky-pilots preach. I ain't never had religion; but I know whatever it is what comes after it can't be no worser'n this. I don't like to leave you, Drisc, but— that's all.

DRISCOLL [*With a groan*] Lad, lad, don't be talkin'.

YANK   This sailor life ain't much to cry about leavin'—just one ship after another, hard work, small pay, and bum grub; and when we git into port, just a drunk endin' up in a fight, and all your money gone, and then ship away again. Never meetin' no nice people; never gittin outa sailor town, hardly, in any port; travellin' all over the world and never seein' none of it; without no one to care whether you're alive or dead. [*With a bitter smile*] There ain't much in all that that'd make yuh sorry to lose it, Drisc.

DRISCOLL [*Gloomily*]   It's a hell av a life, the sea.

YANK [*Musingly*]   It must be great to stay on dry land all your life and have a farm with a house of your own with cows and pigs and chickens, 'way in the middle of the land where yuh'd never smell the sea or see a ship. It must be great to have a wife, and kids to play with at night after supper when your work was done. It must be great to have a home of your own, Drisc.

DRISCOLL [*With a great sigh*]   It must, surely; but what's the use av thinkin' av ut? Such things are not for the loikes av us.

YANK   Sea-farin' is all right when you're young and don't care, but we ain't chickens no more, and somehow, I dunno, this last year has seemed rotten, and I've had a hunch I'd quit—with you, of course

—and we'd save our coin, and go to Canada or Argentine or some place and git a farm, just a small one, just enough to live on. I never told yuh this cause I thought you'd laugh at me.

DRISCOLL [*Enthusiastically*]   Laugh at you, is ut? When I'm havin' the same thoughts myself, toime afther toime. It's a grand idea and we'll be doin' ut sure if you'll stop your crazy notions—about—about bein' so sick.

YANK [*Sadly*]   Too late. We shouldn'ta made this trip, and then—— How'd all the fog git in here?

DRISCOLL   Fog?

YANK   Everything looks misty. Must be my eyes gittin' weak, I guess. What was we talkin' of a minute ago? Oh, yes, a farm. It's too late. [*His mind wandering*] Argentine, did I say? D'yuh remember the times we've had in Buenos Aires? The moving pictures in Barracas? Some class to them, d'yuh remember?

DRISCOLL [*With satisfaction*]   I do that; and so does the piany player. He'll not be forgettin' the black eye I gave him in a hurry.

YANK   Remember the time we was there on the beach and had to go to Tommy Moore's boarding house to git shipped? And he sold us rotten oilskins and seaboots full of holes, and shipped us on a skysail yarder round the Horn, and took two months' pay for it. And the days we used to sit on the park benches along the Paseo Colon with the vigilantes lookin' hard at us? And the songs at the Sailor's Opera where the guy played ragtime—d'yuh remember them?

DRISCOLL   I do, surely.

YANK   And La Plata—phew, the stink of the hides! I always liked Argentine—all except that booze, caña. How drunk we used to git on that, remember?

DRISCOLL   Cud I forget ut? My head pains me at the menshun av that divil's brew.

YANK   Remember the night I went crazy with the heat in Singapore? And the time you was pinched by the cops in Port Said? And the time we was both locked up in Sydney for fightin'?

DRISCOLL   I do so.

YANK   And that fight on the dock at Cape Town —— [*His voice betrays great inward perturbation.*]

DRISCOLL [*Hastily*]   Don't be thinkin' av that now. 'Tis past and gone.

YANK   D'yuh think He'll hold it up against me?

DRISCOLL [*Mystified*]   Who's that?

YANK   God. They say He sees everything. He must know it was done in fair fight, in self-defense, don't yuh think?

DRISCOLL   Av course. Ye stabbed him, and be damned to him, for the skulkin' swine he was, afther him tryin' to stick you in the back, and you not suspectin'. Let your conscience be aisy. I wisht I had nothin' blacker than that on my sowl. I'd not be afraid av the angel Gabriel himself.

YANK [*With a shudder*]   I c'd see him a minute ago with the blood spurtin' out of his neck. Ugh!

DRISCOLL   The fever, ut is, that makes you see such things. Give no heed to ut.

YANK [*Uncertainly*] You don't think He'll hold it up agin me—God, I mean.

DRISCOLL If there's justice in hiven, no! [YANK *seems comforted by this assurance.*]

YANK [*After a pause*] We won't reach Cardiff for a week at least. I'll be buried at sea.

DRISCOLL [*Putting his hands over his ears*] Ssshh! I won't listen to you.

YANK [*As if he had not heard him*] It's as good a place as any other, I s'pose—only I always wanted to be buried on dry land. But what the hell'll I care then? [*Fretfully*] Why should it be a rotten night like this with that damned whistle blowin' and people snorin' all round? I wish the stars was out, and the moon, too; I c'd lie out on deck and look at them, and it'd make it easier to go—somehow.

DRISCOLL For the love av God don't be talkin' loike that!

YANK Whatever pay's comin' to me yuh can divvy up with the rest of the boys; and you take my watch. It ain't worth much, but it's all I've got.

DRISCOLL But have ye no relations at all to call your own?

YANK No, not as I know of. One thing I forgot: You know Fanny the barmaid at the Red Stork in Cardiff?

DRISCOLL Sure, and who doesn't?

YANK She's been good to me. She tried to lend me half a crown when I was broke there last trip. Buy her the biggest box of candy yuh c'n find in Cardiff. [*Breaking down—in a choking voice*] It's

hard to ship on this voyage I'm goin' on—alone!
[DRISCOLL *reaches out and grasps his hand. There
is a pause, during which both fight to control themselves.*] My throat's like a furnace. [*He gasps for air.*]
Gimme a drink of water, will yuh, Drisc? [DRISCOLL
gets him a dipper of water.] I wish this was a pint
of beer. Oooohh! [*He chokes, his face convulsed
with agony, his hands tearing at his shirt front. The
dipper falls from his nerveless fingers.*]

DRISCOLL   For the love av God, what is ut, Yank?

YANK [*Speaking with tremendous difficulty*]
S'long, Drisc! [*He stares straight in front of him
with eyes starting from their sockets.*] Who's that?

DRISCOLL   Who? What?

YANK [*Faintly*]   A pretty lady dressed in black.
[*His face twitches and his body writhes in a final
spasm, then straightens out rigidly.*]

DRISCOLL [*Pale with horror*]   Yank! Yank! Say a
word to me for the love av hiven! [*He shrinks away
from the bunk, making the sign of the cross. Then
comes back and puts a trembling hand on* YANK's
chest and bends closely over the body.]

COCKY [*From the alleyway*]   Oh, Driscoll! Can
you leave Yank for arf a mo' and give me a 'and?

DRISCOLL [*With a great sob*]   Yank! [*He sinks
down on his knees beside the bunk, his head on his
hands. His lips move in some half-remembered
prayer.*]

COCKY [*Enters, his oilskins and sou'wester glis-
tening with drops of water*]   The fog's lifted.
[COCKY *sees* DRISCOLL *and stands staring at him*

with open mouth. DRISCOLL *makes the sign of the cross again.*]

COCKY [*Mockingly*] Sayin' 'is prayers! [*He catches sight of the still figure in the bunk and an expression of awed understanding comes over his face. He takes off his dripping sou'wester and stands, scratching his head.*]

COCKY [*In a hushed whisper*]   Gawd blimey!

[*The curtain falls.*]

THE LONG
VOYAGE HOME

A Play in One Act

CHARACTERS

FAT JOE, *proprietor of a dive*
NICK, *a crimp*
MAG, *a barmaid*
Seamen of the British tramp steamer **Glencairn**
    OLSON
    DRISCOLL
    COCKY
    IVAN
KATE
FREDA
TWO ROUGHS

THE LONG
VOYAGE HOME

SCENE *The bar of a low dive on the London water front—a squalid, dingy room dimly lighted by kerosene lamps placed in brackets on the walls. On the left, the bar. In front of it, a door leading to a side room. On the right, tables with chairs around them. In the rear, a door leading to the street.*

A slovenly barmaid with a stupid face sodden with drink is mopping off the bar. Her arm moves back and forth mechanically and her eyes are half shut as if she were dozing on her feet. At the far end of the bar stands FAT JOE, *the proprietor, a gross bulk of a man with an enormous stomach. His face is red and bloated, his little piggish eyes being almost concealed by rolls of fat. The thick fingers of his big hands are loaded with cheap rings and a gold watch chain of cable-like proportions stretches across his checked waistcoat.*

At one of the tables, front, a round-shoul-

*dered young fellow is sitting, smoking a ciga-
rette. His face is pasty, his mouth weak, his
eyes shifting and cruel. He is dressed in a
shabby suit, which must have once been
cheaply flashy, and wears a muffler and cap.*

It is about nine o'clock in the evening.

JOE [*Yawning*] Blimey if bizness ain't 'arf slow
to-night. I donnow wot's 'appened. The place is like
a bleedin' tomb. Where's all the sailor men, I'd like
to know? [*Raising his voice*] Ho, you Nick! [NICK
turns around listlessly.] Wot's the name o' that
wessel put in at the dock below jest arter noon?

NICK [*Laconically*] Glencairn—from Bewnezerry
[Buenos Aires].

JOE Ain't the crew been paid orf yet?

NICK Paid orf this arternoon, they tole me. I
'opped on board of 'er an' seen 'em. 'Anded 'em
some o' yer cards, I did. They promised faithful
they'd 'appen in to-night—them as whose time was
done.

JOE Any two-year men to be paid orf?

NICK Four—three Britishers an' a square-'ead.

JOE [*Indignantly*] An' yer popped orf an' left
'em? An' me a-payin' yer to 'elp an' bring 'em in
'ere!

NICK [*Grumblingly*] Much you pays me! An' I
ain't slingin' me 'ook abaht the 'ole bleedin' town
fur now man. See?

JOE I ain't speakin' on'y fur meself. Down't I
always give yer yer share, fair an' square, as man to
man?

NICK [*With a sneer*]   Yus—b'cause you 'as to.

JOE   'As to? Listen to 'im! There's many'd be 'appy to 'ave your berth, me man!

NICK   Yes? Wot wiv the peelers li'ble to put me away in the bloody jail fur crimpin', an' all?

JOE [*Indignantly*]   We down't do no crimpin'.

NICK [*Sarcastically*]   Ho, now! Not 'arf!

JOE [*A bit embarrassed*]   Well, on'y a bit now an' agen when there ain't no reg'lar trade. [*To hide his confusion he turns to the barmaid angrily. She is still mopping off the bar, her chin on her breast, half-asleep.*] 'Ere, me gel, we've 'ad enough o' that. You been a-moppin', an' a-moppin', an' a-moppin' the blarsted bar fur a 'ole 'our. 'Op it aht o' this! You'd fair guv a bloke the shakes a-watchin' yer.

MAG [*Beginning to sniffle*]   Ow, you do frighten me when you 'oller at me, Joe. I ain't a bad gel, I ain't. Gawd knows I tries to do me best fur you. [*She bursts into a tempest of sobs.*]

JOE [*Roughly*]   Stop yer grizzlin'! An' 'op it aht of 'ere!

NICK [*Chuckling*]   She's drunk, Joe. Been 'ittin' the gin, eh, Mag?

MAG [*Ceases crying at once and turns on him furiously*]   You little crab, you! Orter wear a muzzle, you ort! A-openin' of your ugly mouth to a 'onest woman what ain't never done you no 'arm [*Commencing to sob again*] H'abusin' me like a dawg cos I'm sick an' orf me oats, an' all.

JOE   Orf yer go, me gel! Go hupstairs and 'ave a sleep. I'll wake yer if I wants yer. An' wake the two gels when yer goes hup. It's 'arpas' nine an' time as some one was a-comin' in, tell 'em. D'yer 'ear me?

MAG [*Stumbling around the bar to the door on left—sobbing*] Yus, yus, I 'ears you. Gawd knows wot's going' to 'appen to me, I'm that sick. Much you cares if I dies, down't you? [*She goes out.*]

JOE [*Still brooding over* NICK's *lack of diligence —after a pause*] Four two-year men paid orf wiv their bloody pockets full o' sovereigns—an' yer lorst 'em. [*He shakes his head sorrowfully.*]

NICK [*Impatiently*] Stow it! They promised faithful they'd come, I tells yer. They'll be walkin' in in 'arf a mo'. There's lots o' time yet. [*In a low voice*] 'Av yer got the drops? We might wanter use 'em.

JOE [*Taking a small bottle from behind the bar*] Yus; 'ere it is.

NICK [*With satisfaction*] Righto! [*His shifty eyes peer about the room searchingly. Then he beckons to* JOE, *who comes over to the table and sits down.*] Reason I arst yer about the drops was 'cause I seen the capt'n of the *Amindra* this arternoon.

JOE The *Amindra*? Wot ship is that?

NICK Bloody windjammer—skys'l yarder—full rigged—painted white—been layin' at the dock above 'ere fur a month. You knows 'er.

JOE Ho, yus. I knows now.

NICK The capt'n says as 'e wants a man special bad—ter-night. They sails at daybreak ter-morrer.

JOE There's plenty o' 'ands lyin' abaht waitin' fur ships, I should fink.

NICK Not fur this ship, ole buck. The capt'n an' mate are bloody slave-drivers, an' they're bound down round the 'Orn. They 'arf starved the 'ands on the larst trip 'ere, an' no one'll dare ship on 'er. [*After a pause*] I promised the capt'n faithful I'd get 'im one, and ter-night.

JOE [*Doubtfully*] An' 'ow are yer goin' to git 'im?

NICK [*With a wink*] I was thinkin' as one of 'em from the *Glencairn*'d do—them as was pair orf an' is comin' 'ere.

JOE [*With a grin*] It'd be a good 'aul, that's the troof. [*Frowning*] If they comes 'ere.

NICK They'll come, an' they'll all be rotten drunk, wait an' see. [*There is the noise of loud, boisterous singing from the street.*] Sounds like 'em, now. [*He opens the street door and looks out.*] Gawd blimey if it ain't the four of 'em! [*Turning to Joe in triumph*] Naw, what d'yer say? They're lookin' for the place. I'll go aht an tell 'em. [*He goes out. Joe gets into position behind the bar, assuming his most oily smile. A moment later the door is opened, admitting* DRISCOLL, COCKY, IVAN *and* OLSEN. DRISCOLL *is a tall, powerful Irishman;* COCKY, *a wizened runt of a man with a straggling gray mustache;* IVAN, *a hulking oaf of a peasant;* OLSON, *a stocky, middle-aged Swede with round, childish blue eyes. The first three are all very drunk, especially* IVAN, *who is managing his legs with difficulty.* OLSON *is perfectly sober. All are dressed in their ill-fitting shore clothes and look very uncomfortable.* DRISCOLL *has unbuttoned his stiff collar*

and its ends stick out sideways. He has lost his tie.
NICK *slinks into the room after them and sits down
at a table in rear. The seamen come to the table,
front.*]

JOE [*With affected heartiness*] Ship ahoy, mates!
'Appy to see yer 'home safe an' sound.

DRISCOLL [*Turns round, swaying a bit, and peers
at him across the bar*] So ut's you, is ut? [*He looks
about the place with an air of recognition.*] 'An the
same damn rat's-hole, sure enough. I remimber
foive or six years back 'twas here I was sthripped av
me last shillin' whin I was aslape. [*With sudden
fury*] God stiffen ye, come none av your dog's
thricks on me this trip or I'll— [*He shakes his fist
at* JOE.]

JOE [*Hastily interrupting*] Yer must be mis-
taiken. This is a 'onest place, this is.

COCKY [*Derisively*] Ho, yus! An' you're a
bleedin' angel, I s'pose?

IVAN [*Vaguely taking off his derby hat and putting it on again—plaintively*] I don' li-ike dis place.

DRISCOLL [*Going over to the bar—as genial as he
was furious a moment before*] Well, no matther,
'tis all past an' gone an' forgot. I'm not the man to
be holdin' harrd feelin's on me first night ashore,
an' me dhrunk as a lord. [*He holds out his hand,
which* JOE *takes very gingerly.*] We'll all be havin' a
dhrink, I'm thinkin'. Whiskey for the three av us—
Irish whiskey!

COCKY [*Mockingly*] An' a glarse o' ginger beer
fur our blarsted love-child 'ere. [*He jerks his thumb
at* OLSON.]

OLSEN [*With a good-natured grin*] I bane a good boy dis night, for one time.

DRISCOLL [*Bellowing, and pointing to* NICK *as* JOE *brings the drinks to the table*] An' see what that crimpin' son av a crimp'll be wantin'—an' have your own pleasure. [*He pulls a sovereign out of his pocket and slams it on the bar.*]

NICK Guv me a pint o' beer, Joe. [JOE *draws the beer and takes it down to the far end of the bar.* NICK *comes over to get it and* JOE *gives him a significant wink and nods toward the door on the left.* NICK *signals back that he understands.*]

COCKY [*Drink in hand—impatiently*] I'm that bloody dry! [*Lifting his glass to* DRISCOLL] Cheero, ole dear, cheero!

DRISCOLL [*Pocketing his change without looking at it*] A toast for ye: Hell roast that divil av a bo'sun! [*He drinks.*]

COCKY Righto! Gawd strike 'im blind! [*He drains his glass.*]

IVAN [*Half-asleep*] Dot's gude. [*He tosses down his drink in one gulp.* OLSEN *sips his ginger ale.* NICK *takes a swallow of his beer and then comes round the bar and goes out the door on left.*]

COCKY [*Producing a sovereign*] Ho there, you Fatty! Guv us another!

JOE The saime, mates?

COCKY Yus.

DRISCOLL No, ye scut! I'll be havin' a pint av beer. I'm dhry as a loime kiln.

IVAN [*Suddenly getting to his feet in a befuddled manner and nearly upsetting the table*] I don' li-ike dis place! I wan' see girls—plenty girls. [*Pathetically*] I don't li-ike dis place. I wan' dance with girl.

DRISCOLL [*Pushing him back on his chair with a thud*] Shut up, ye Rooshan baboon! A foine Romeo you'd make in your condishun. [IVAN *blubbers some incoherent protest—then suddenly falls asleep.*]

JOE [*Bringing the drinks—looks at* OLSON] An' you, matey?

OLSON [*Shaking his head*] Noting dis time, thank you.

COCKY [*Mockingly*] A-saivin' of 'is money, 'e is! Goin' back to 'ome an' mother. Goin' to buy a bloomin' farm an' punch the blarsted dirt, that's wot 'e is! [*Spitting disgustedly*] There's a funny bird of a sailor man for yer, Gawd blimey!

OLSEN [*Wearing the same good-natured grin*] Yust what I like, Cocky. I wus on farm long time when I wus kid.

DRISCOLL   Lave him alone, ye bloody insect! 'Tis a foine sight to see a man wid some sense in his head instead av a damn fool the loike av us. I only wisht I'd a mother alive to call me own. I'd not be dhrunk in this divil's hole this minute, maybe.

COCKY [*Commencing to weep dolorously*] Ow, down't talk, Drisc! I can't bear to 'ear you. I ain't never 'ad no mother, I ain't——

DRISCOLL   Shut up, ye ape, an' don't be makin' that squealin'. If ye cud see your ugly face, wid the big red nose av ye all screwed up in a knot, ye'd never shed a tear the rist av your loife. [*Roaring into song*] We ar-re the byes av We-e-exford who fought wid hearrt an' hand! [*Speaking*] To hell wid Ulster! [*He drinks and the others follow his example.*] An' I'll strip to any man in the city av London won't dhrink to that toast. [*He glares truculently at* Joe, *who immediately downs his beer.* Nick *enters again from the door on the left and comes up to* Joe *and whispers in his ear. The latter nods with satisfaction.*]

Driscoll [*Glowering at them*] What divil's thrick are ye up to now, the two av ye? [*He flourishes a brawny fist.*] Play fair wid us or ye deal wid me!

Joe [*Hastily*] No trick, shipmate! May Gawd kill me if that ain't troof!

Nick [*Indicating* Ivan, *who is snoring*] On'y your mate there was arskin' fur gels an' I thorght as 'ow yer'd like 'em to come dawhn and 'ave a wet wiv yer.

Joe [*With a smirking wink*] Pretty, 'olesome gels they be, ain't they, Nick?"

Nick   Yus.

Cocky   Aar! I knows the gels you 'as, not 'arf! They'd fair blind yer, they're that 'omely. None of yer bloomin' gels fur me, ole Fatty. Me an' Drisc knows a place, down't we, Drisc?"

Driscoll   Divil a lie, we do. An' we'll be afther goin' there in a minute. There's music there an' a bit av a dance to liven a man.

Joe   Nick, 'ere, can play yer a tune, can't yer, Nick?

Nick   Yus.

JOE   An' yer can 'ave a dance in the side room 'ere.

DRISCOLL   Hurroo! Now you're talkin'. [*The two women,* FREDA *and* KATE, *enter from the left.* FREDA *is a little, sallow-faced blonde.* KATE *is stout and dark.*]

COCKY [*In a loud aside to* DRISCOLL] Gawd blimey, look at 'em! Ain't they 'orrible? [*The women come forward to the table, wearing their best set smiles.*]

FREDA [*In a raspy voice*] 'Ullo, mates.

KATE   'Ad a good voyage?

DRISCOLL   Rotten; but no matther. Welcome, as the sayin' is, an' sit down, an' what'll ye be takin' for your thirst? [*To* KATE] You'll be sittin' by me, darlin'—what's your name?

KATE [*With a stupid grin*] Kate. [*She stands by his chair.*]

DRISCOLL [*Putting his arm around her*] A good Irish name, but you're English by the trim av ye, an' be damned to you. But no matter. Ut's fat ye are, Katy dear, an' I never cud endure skinny wimin. [FREDA *favors him with a viperish glance and sits by* OLSON.] What'll ye have?

OLSON   No, Drisc. Dis one bane on me. [*He takes out a roll of notes from his inside pocket and lays one on the table.* JOE, NICK, *and the women look at the money with greedy eyes.* IVAN *gives a particularly violent snore.*]

FREDA   Waike up your fren'. Gawd, 'ow I 'ates to 'ear snorin'.

DRISCOLL [*Springing to action, smashes* IVAN's *derby over his ears*] D'you hear the lady talkin' to ye, ye Rooshan swab? [*The only reply to this is a snore.* DRISCOLL *pulls the battered remains of the derby off* IVAN's *head and smashes it back again.*] Arise an' shine, ye dhrunken swine! [*Another snore. The women giggle.* DRISCOLL *throws the beer left in his glass into* IVAN's *face. The Russian comes to in a flash, spluttering. There is a roar of laughter.*]

IVAN [*Indignantly*] I tell you—dot's someting I don' li-ike!

COCKY Down't waste good beer, Drisc.

IVAN [*Grumblingly*] I tell you—dot is not ri-ight.

DRISCOLL Ut's your own doin', Ivan. Ye was moanin' for girrls an' whin they come you sit gruntin' loike a pig in a sty. Have ye no manners? [IVAN *seems to see the women for the first time and grins foolishly.*]

KATE [*Laughing at him*] Cheero, ole chum, 'ow's Russha?

IVAN [*Greatly pleased—putting his hand in his pocket*] I buy a drink.

OLSON No; dis one bane on me. [*To* JOE] Hey, you faller!

JOE Wot'll it be, Kate?

KATE Gin.

FREDA Brandy.

DRISCOLL An' Irish whiskey for the rist av us—wid the excipshun av our timperance friend, God pity him!

FREDA [*To* OLSON] You ain't drinkin'?

OLSON [*Half-ashamed*]   No.

FREDA [*With a seductive smile*]   I down't blame yer. You got sense, you 'ave. I on'y tike a nip o' brandy now an' agen fur my 'ealth. [JOE *brings the drinks and* OLSON'S *change.* COCKY *gets unsteadily to his feet and raises his glass in the air.*]

COCKY   'Ere's a toff toast for yer: The ladies, Gawd—[*He hesitates—then adds in a grudging tone*]—bless 'em.

KATE [*With a silly giggle*]   Oo-er! That wasn't what you was goin' to say, you bad Cocky, you! [*They all drink.*]

DRISCOLL [*To* NICK]   Where's the tune ye was promisin' to give us?

NICK   Come ahn in the side 'ere an' you'll 'ear it.

DRISCOLL [*Getting up*]   Come on, all av ye. We'll have a tune an' a dance if I'm not too dhrunk to dance, God help me. [COCKY *and* IVAN *stagger to their feet.* IVAN *can hardly stand. He is leering at* KATE *and snickering to himself in a maudlin fashion. The three, led by* NICK, *go out the door on the left.* KATE *follows them.* OLSON *and* FREDA *remain seated.*]

COCKY [*Calling over his shoulder*]   Come on an' dance, Ollie.

OLSON   Yes, I come. [*He starts to get up. From the side room comes the sound of an accordion and a boisterous whoop from* DRISCOLL, *followed by a heavy stamping of feet.*]

FREDA   Ow, down't go in there. Stay 'ere an' 'ave a talk wiv me. They're all drunk an' you ain't drinkin'. [*With a smile up into his face*] I'll think yer don't like me if yer goes in there.

OLSON [*Confused*]   You wus wrong, Miss Freda. I don't—I mean I do like you.

FREDA [*Smiling—puts her hand over his on the table*]   An' I likes you. Yer a genelman. You don't get drunk an' hinsult poor gels wot 'as a 'ard an' uneppy life.

OLSON [*Pleased but still more confused—wriggling his feet*]   I bane drunk many time, Miss Freda.

FREDA   Then why ain't yer drinkin' now? [*She exchanges a quick, questioning glance with* JOE, *who nods back at her—then she continues persuasively*] Tell me somethin' abaht yeself.

OLSON [*With a grin*]   There ain't noting to say, Miss Freda. I bane poor devil sailor man, dat's all.

FREDA   Where was you born—Norway? [OLSON *shakes his head.*] Denmark?

OLSON   No. You guess once more.

FREDA   Then it must be Sweden.

OLSON   Yes. I wus born in Stockholm.

FREDA [*Pretending great delight*]   Ow, ain't that funny! I was born there, too—in Stockholm.

OLSON [*Astonished*]   You wus born in Sweden?

FREDA   Yes; you wouldn't think it, but it's Gawd's troof. [*She claps her hands delightedly.*]

OLSON [*Beaming all over*]   You speak Swedish?

FREDA [*Trying to smile sadly*]   Now. Y'see my ole man an' woman come 'ere to England when I was on'y a baby an' they was speakin' English b'fore

I was old enough to learn. Sow I never knew Swedish. [*Sadly*] Wisht I 'ad! [*With a smile*] We'd 'ave a bloomin' lark of it if I 'ad, wouldn't we?

OLSON It sound nice to hear the old talk yust once in a time.

FREDA Righto! No place like yer 'ome, I says. Are yer goin' up to—to Stockholm b'fore yer ships away agen?

OLSON Yes. I go home from here to Stockholm. [*Proudly*] As passenger!

FREDA An' you'll git another ship up there arter you've 'ad a vacation?

OLSON No. I don't never ship on sea no more. I got all sea want for my life—too much hard work for little money. Yust work, work, work on ship. I don't want more.

FREDA Ow, I see. That's why you give up drinkin'.

OLSON Yes. [*With a grin*] If I drink I yust get drunk and spend all money.

FREDA But if you ain't gointer be a sailor no more, what'll yer do? You been a sailor all yer life, ain't yer?

OLSON No. I work on farm till I am eighteen. I like it, too—it's nice—work on farm.

FREDA But ain't Stockholm a city same's London? Ain't no farm there, is there?

OLSON We live—my brother and mother live—my father iss dead—on farm yust a little way from Stockholm. I have plenty money, now. I go back with two years' pay and buy more land yet; work on farm. [*Grinning*] No more sea, no more bum grub, no more storms—yust nice work.

FREDA Ow, ain't that luv'ly! I s'pose you'll be gittin' married, too?

OLSON [*Very much confused*] I don't know. I like to, if I find nice girl, maybe.

FREDA Ain't yer got some gel back in Stockholm? I bet yer 'as.

OLSON No. I got nice girl once before I go on sea. But I go on ship, and I don't come back, and she marry other faller. [*He grins sheepishly.*]

FREDA Well, it's nice for yer to be goin' 'ome, anyway.

OLSON Yes. I tank so. [*There is a crash from the room on left and the music abruptly stops. A moment later* COCKY *and* DRISCOLL *appear, supporting the inert form of* IVAN *between them. He is in the last stage of intoxication, unable to move a muscle.* NICK *follows them and sits down at the table in rear.*]

DRISCOLL [*As they zigzag up to the bar*] Ut's dead he is, I'm thinkin', for he's as limp as a blarsted corpse.

COCKY [*Puffing*] Gawd, 'e ain't 'arf 'eavy!

DRISCOLL [*Slapping* IVAN's *face with his free hand*] Wake up, ye divil, ye. Ut's no use. Gabriel's trumpet itself cudn't rouse him. [*To* JOE] Give us a dhrink for I'm perishing wid the thirst. 'Tis harrd worrk, this.

JOE Whiskey?

DRISCOLL *Irish* whiskey, ye swab. [*He puts down*

a coin on the bar. JOE *serves* COCKY *and* DRISCOLL. *They drink and then swerve over to* OLSON's *table.*]

OLSON Sit down and rest for time, Drisc.

DRISCOLL No, Ollie, we'll be takin' this lad home to his bed. Ut's late for wan so young to be out in the night. An' I'd not trust him in this hole as dhrunk as he is, an' him wid a full pay day on him. [*Shaking his fist at* JOE] Oho, I know your games, me sonny bye!

JOE [*With an air of grievance*] There yer goes again—hinsultin' a 'onest man!

COCKY Ho, listen to 'im! Guv 'im a shove in the marf, Drisc.

OLSON [*Anxious to avoid a fight—getting up*] I help you take Ivan to boarding house.

FREDA [*Protestingly*] Ow, you ain't gointer leave me, are yer? An' we 'avin' sech a nice talk, an' all.

DRISCOLL [*With a wink*] Ye hear what the lady says, Ollie. Ye'd best stay here, me timperance lady's man. An' we need no help. 'Tis only a bit av a way and we're two strong men if we are dhrunk. Ut's no hard shift to take the remains home. But ye can open the door for us, Ollie. [OLSON *goes to the door and opens it.*] Come on, Cocky, an' don't be fallin' aslape yourself. [*They lurch toward the door. As they go out* DRISCOLL *shouts back over his shoulder.*] We'll be comin' back in a short time, surely. So wait here for us, Ollie.

OLSON All right. I wait here, Drisc. [*He stands in the doorway uncertainly.* JOE *makes violent signs to* FREDA *to bring him back. She goes over and puts her arm around* OLSON's *shoulder.* JOE *motions to*

NICK *to come to the bar. They whisper together excitedly.*]

FREDA [*Coaxingly*] You ain't gointer leave me, are yer, dearie? [*Then irritably*] Fur Gawd's sake, shet that door! I'm fair freezin' to death wiv the fog. [OLSON *comes to himself with a start and shuts the door.*]

OLSON [*Humbly*] Excuse me, Miss Freda.

FREDA [*Leading him back to the table—coughing*] Buy me a drink o' brandy, will yer? I'm sow cold.

OLSON All you want, Miss Freda, all you want. [*To* JOE, *who is still whispering instructions to* NICK] Hey, Yoe! Brandy for Miss Freda. [*He lays a coin on the table.*]

JOE Righto! [*He pours out her drink and brings it to the table.*] 'Avin' somethink yeself, shipmate?

OLSON No. I don't tank so. [*He points to his glass with a grin.*] Dis iss only belly-wash, no? [*He laughs.*]

JOE [*Hopefully*] 'Ave a man's drink.

OLSON I would like to—but no. If I drink one I want drink one tousand. [*He laughs again.*]

FREDA [*Responding to a vicious nudge from* JOE'S *elbow*] Ow, tike somethin'. I ain't gointer drink all by meself.

OLSEN Den give me a little yinger beer—small one. [JOE *goes back of the bar, making a sign to* NICK *to go to their table.* NICK *does so and stands so that the sailor cannot see what* JOE *is doing.*]

NICK [*To make talk*] Where's yer mates popped orf ter? [JOE *pours the contents of the little bottle into* OLSON's *glass of ginger beer.*]

OLSON   Dey take Ivan, dat drunk faller, to bed. They come back. [JOE *brings* OLSON'S *drink to the table and sets it before him.*]

JOE [*To* NICK—*angrily*] 'Op it, will yer? There ain't no time to be dawdlin'. See? 'Urry!

NICK   Down't worry, ole bird, I'm orf. [*He hurries out the door.* JOE *returns to his place behind the bar.*]

OLSON [*After a pause—worriedly*] I tank I should go after dem. Cocky iss very drunk, too, and Drisc—

FREDA   Aar! The big Irish is all right. Don't yer 'ear 'im say as 'ow they'd surely come back 'ere, an' fur you to wait fur 'em?

OLSON   Yes; but if dey don't come soon I tank I go see if dey are in boarding house all right.

FREDA   Where is the boardin' 'ouse?

OLSON   Yust little way back from street here.

FREDA   You stayin' there, too?

OLSON   Yes—until steamer sail for Stockholm—in two day.

FREDA [*She is alternately looking at* JOE *and feverishly trying to keep* OLSON *talking so he will forget about going away after the others*] Yer mother won't be arf glad to see yer agen, will she? [OLSON *smiles.*] Does she know yer comin'?

OLSON   No. I tought I would yust give her surprise. I wrote to her from Bonos Eres but I don't tell her I come home.

FREDA   Must be old, ain't she, yer ole lady?

OLSON   She iss eighty-two. [*He smiles reminiscently.*] You know, Miss Freda, I don't see my mother or my brother in—let me tank— [*He counts laboriously on his fingers*] must be more than ten year. I write once in while and she write many time; and my brother he write me, too. My mother say in all letter I should come home right away. My brother he write same ting, too. He want me to help him on farm. I write back always I come soon; and I mean all time to go back home at end of voyage. But I come ashore, I take one drink, I take many drinks, I get drunk, I spend all money, I have to ship away for other voyage. So dis time I say to myself: Don't drink one drink, Ollie, or, sure, you don't get home. And I want go home dis time. I feel homesick for farm and to see my people again. [*He smiles.*] Yust like little boy, I feel homesick. Dat's why I don't drink noting to-night but dis— belly-wash! [*He roars with childish laughter, then suddenly becomes serious.*] You know, Miss Freda, my mother get very old, and I want see her. She might die and I would never—

FREDA [*Moved a lot in spite of herself*] Ow, don't talk like that! I jest 'ates to 'ear any one speakin' abaht dyin'. [*The door to the street is opened and* NICK *enters, followed by two rough-looking, shabbily-dressed men, wearing mufflers, with caps pulled down over their eyes. They sit at the table nearest to the door.* JOE *brings them three beers, and there is a whispered consultation, with many glances in the direction of* OLSON.]

OLSON [*Starting to get up—worriedly*] I tank I go round to boarding house. I tank someting go wrong with Drisc and Cocky.

FREDA   Ow, down't go. They kin take care of theyselves. They ain't babies. Wait 'arf a mo'. You ain't 'ad yer drink yet.

JOE [*Coming hastily over to the table, indicates the men in the rear with a jerk of his thumb*]   One of them blokes wants yer to 'ave a wet wiv 'im.

FREDA   Righto! [*To* OLSON] Let's drink this. [*She raises her glass. He does the same.*] 'Ere's a toast fur yer: Success to yer bloomin' farm an' may yer live long an' 'appy on it. Skoal! [*She tosses down her brandy. He swallows half his glass of ginger beer and makes a wry face.*]

OLSON   Skoal! [*He puts down his glass.*]

FREDA [*With feigned indignation*]   Down't yer like my toast?

OLSON [*Grinning*]   Yes. It iss very kind, Miss Freda.

FREDA   Then drink it all like I done.

OLSON   Well—— [*He gulps down the rest.*] Dere! [*He laughs.*]

FREDA   Done like a sport!

ONE OF THE ROUGHS [*With a laugh*]   Amindra, ahoy!

NICK [*Warningly*]   Sssshh!

OLSON [*Turns around in his chair*]   Amindra? Iss she in port? I sail on her once long time ago—three mast, full rig, skys'l yarder? Iss dat ship you mean?

THE ROUGH [*Grinning*]   Yus; right you are.

OLSON [*Angrily*]   I know dat damn ship—worst ship dat sail to sea. Rotten grub and dey make you work all time—and the Captain and Mate wus Bluenose devils. No sailor who know anyting ever ship on her. Where iss she bound from here?

THE ROUGH   Round Cape 'Orn—sails at daybreak.

OLSON   Py yingo, I pity poor fallers make dat trip round Cape Stiff dis time year. I bet you some of dem never see port once again. [*He passes his hand over his eyes in a dazed way. His voice grows weaker.*] Py golly, I feel dizzy. All the room go round and round like I wus drunk. [*He gets weakly to his feet.*] Good night, Miss Freda. I bane feeling sick. Tell Drisc—I go home. [*He takes a step forward and suddenly collapses over a chair, rolls to the floor, and lies there unconscious.*]

JOE [*From behind the bar*]   Quick, nawh! [NICK *darts forward with* JOE *following.* FREDA *is already beside the unconscious man and has taken the roll of money from his inside pocket. She strips off a note furtively and shoves it into her bosom, trying to conceal her action, but* JOE *sees her. She hands the roll to* JOE, *who pockets it.* NICK *goes through all the other pockets and lays a handful of change on the table.*]

JOE [*Impatiently*]   'Urry, 'urry, can't yer? The other blokes'll be 'ere in 'arf a mo'. [*The two roughs come forward.*] 'Ere, you two, tike 'im in under the arms like 'e was drunk. [*They do so.*] Tike 'im to the *Amindra*—yer knows that, don't yer?—two docks above. Nick'll show yer. An' you, Nick, down't yer leave the bleedin' ship till the capt'n guvs yer this bloke's advance—full month's pay—five quid, d'yer 'ear?

NICK   I knows me bizness, ole bird. [*They support* OLSON *to the door.*]

THE ROUGH [*As they are going out*]   This silly bloke'll 'ave the s'prise of 'is life when 'e wakes up on board of 'er. [*They laugh. The door closes behind them.* FREDA *moves quickly for the door on the left but* JOE *gets in her way and stops her.*]

JOE [*Threateningly*]   Guv us what yer took!

FREDA   Took? I guv yer all 'e 'ad.

JOE   Yer a liar! I seen yer a-playin' yer sneakin' tricks, but yer can't fool Joe. I'm too old a 'and. [*Furiously*] Guv it to me, yer bloody cow! [*He grabs her by the arm.*]

FREDA   Lemme alone! I ain't got no—

JOE [*Hits her viciously on the side of the jaw. She crumples up on the floor*]   That'll learn yer! [*He stoops down and fumbles in her bosom and pulls out the banknote, which he stuffs into his pocket with a grunt of satisfaction.* KATE *opens the door on the left and looks in—then rushes to* FREDA *and lifts her head up in her arms.*]

KATE [*Gently*]   Pore dearie! [*Looking at* JOE *angrily*] Been 'ittin' 'er agen, 'ave yer, yer cowardly swine!

JOE   Yus; an' I'll 'it you, too, if yer don't keep yer marf shut. Tike 'er aht of 'ere! [KATE *carries* FREDA *into the next room.* JOE *goes behind the bar. A moment later the outer door is opened and* DRISCOLL *and* COCKY *come in.*]

DRISCOLL   Come on, Ollie. [*He suddenly sees that* OLSON *is not there, and turns to* JOE.] Where is ut he's gone to?

JOE [*With a meaning wink*]   'E an' Freda went aht t'gether 'bout five minutes past. 'E's fair gone on 'er, 'e is.

DRISCOLL [*With a grin*]   Oho, so that's ut, is ut? Who'd think Ollie'd be sich a divil wid the wimin? 'Tis lucky he's sober or she'd have him stripped to his last ha'penny. [*Turning to* COCKY, *who is blinking sleepily*] What'll ye have, ye little scut? [*To* JOE] Give me whiskey, *Irish* whiskey!

[*The curtain falls.*]

IN THE ZONE

A Play in One Act

CHARACTERS

Seamen on the British tramp steamer Glencairn

SMITTY

DAVIS

SWANSON

SCOTTY

IVAN

PAUL

JACK

DRISCOLL

COCKY

IN THE ZONE

SCENE *The seamen's forecastle. On the right above the bunks three or four portholes covered with black cloth can be seen. On the floor near the doorway is a pail with a tin dipper. A lantern in the middle of the floor, turned down very low, throws a dim light around the place. Five men, SCOTTY, IVAN, SWANSON, SMITTY and PAUL, are in their bunks apparently asleep. It is about ten minutes of twelve on a night in the fall of the year 1915.*

SMITTY turns slowly in his bunk and, leaning out over the side, looks from one to another of the men as if to assure himself that they are asleep. Then he climbs carefully out of his bunk and stands in the middle of the forecastle fully dressed, but in his stocking feet, glancing around him suspiciously. Reassured, he leans down and cautiously pulls out a suit-case from under the bunks in front of him.

Just at this moment DAVIS appears in the

doorway, carrying a large steaming coffee-pot in his hand. He stops short when he sees SMITTY. *A puzzled expression comes over his face, followed by one of suspicion, and he retreats farther back in the alleyway, where he can watch* SMITTY *without being seen.*

All the latter's movements indicate a fear of discovery. He takes out a small bunch of keys and unlocks the suit-case, making a slight noise as he does so. SCOTTY *wakes up and peers at him over the side of the bunk.* SMITTY *opens the suit-case and takes out a small black tin box, carefully places this under his mattress, shoves the suit-case back under the bunk, climbs into his bunk again, closes his eyes and begins to snore loudly.*

DAVIS *enters the forecastle, places the coffeepot beside the lantern, and goes from one to the other of the sleepers and shakes them vigorously, saying to each in a low voice:* Near eight bells, Scotty. Arise and shine, Swanson. Eight bells, Ivan. SMITTY *yawns loudly with a great pretense of having been dead asleep. All of the rest of the men tumble out of their bunks, stretching and gaping, and commence to pull on their shoes. They go one by one to the cupboard near the door, take out their cups and spoons, and sit down together on the benches. The coffeepot is passed around. They munch their biscuits and sip their coffee in dull silence.*

DAVIS [*Suddenly jumping to his feet—nervously*] Where's that air comin' from? [*All are startled and look at him wonderingly.*]

SWANSON [*A squat, surly-faced Swede—grumpily*] What air? I don't feel nothing.

DAVIS [*Excitedly*]   I kin feel it—a draft. [*He stands on the bench and looks around—suddenly exploding*] Damn fool square-head! [*He leans over the upper bunk in which* PAUL *is sleeping and slams the port-hole shut.*] I got a good notion to report him. Serve him bloody well right! What's the use o' blindin' the ports when that thick-head goes an' leaves 'em open?

SWANSON [*Yawning—too sleepy to be aroused by anything—carelessly*]   Dey don't see what little light go out yust one port.

SCOTTY [*Protestingly*]   Dinna be a loon, Swanson! D'ye no ken the dangerr o' showin' a licht wi' a pack o' submarrines lyin' aboot?

IVAN [*Shaking his shaggy ox-like head in an emphatic affirmative*]   Dot's right, Scotty. I don' li-ike blow up, no, by devil!

SMITTY [*His manner slightly contemptuous*]   I don't think there's much danger of meeting any of their submarines, not until we get into the war zone, at any rate.

DAVIS [*He and* SCOTTY *look at* SMITTY *suspiciously —harshly*]   You don't, eh? [*He lowers his voice and speaks slowly.*] Well, we're in the war zone right this minit if you wants to know. [*The effect of this speech is instantaneous. All sit bolt upright on their benches and stare at Davis.*]

SMITTY How do you know, Davis?

DAVIS [*Angrily*] 'Cos Drisc heard the First send the Third below to wake the skipper when we fetched the zone—'bout five bells, it was. Now whata y' got to say?

SMITTY [*Conciliatingly*] Oh, I wasn't doubting your word, Davis; but you know they're not pasting up bulletins to let the crew know when the zone is reached—especially on ammunition ships like this.

IVAN [*Decidedly*] I don't li-ike dees voyage. Next time I ship on windjammer Boston to River Plate, load with wood only so it float, by golly!

SWANSON [*Fretfully*] I hope British navy blow 'em to hell, those submarines, py damn!

SCOTTY [*Looking at* SMITTY, *who is staring at the doorway in a dream, his chin on his hands. Meaningly*] It is no the submarrines only we've to fear, I'm thinkin'.

DAVIS [*Assenting eagerly*] That's no lie, Scotty.

SWANSON You mean the mines?

SCOTTY I wasna thinkin' o' mines eitherr.

DAVIS There's many a good ship blown up and at the bottom of the sea, what never hit no mine or torpedo.

SCOTTY Did ye neverr read of the Gerrman spies and the dirrty work they're doin' all the war? [*He and* DAVIS *both glance at* SMITTY, *who is deep in thought and is not listening to the conversation.*]

DAVIS An' the clever way they fool you!

SWANSON Sure; I read it in paper many time.

DAVIS Well—[*He is about to speak but hesitates*

and finishes lamely] you got to watch out, that's all I says.

IVAN [*Drinking the last of his coffee and slamming his fist on the bench explosively*] I tell you dis rotten coffee give me belly-ache, yes! [*They all look at him in amused disgust.*]

SCOTTY [*Sardonically*] Dinna fret about it, Ivan. If we blow up ye'll no be mindin' the pain in your middle. [JACK *enters. He is a young American with a tough, good-natured face. He wears dungarees and a heavy jersey.*]

JACK Eight bells, fellers.

IVAN [*Stupidly*] I don' hear bell ring.

JACK No, and yuh won't hear any ring, yuh boob—[*Lowering his voice unconsciously*] now we're in the war zone.

SWANSON [*Anxiously*] Is the boats all ready?

JACK Sure; we can lower 'em in a second.

DAVIS A lot o' good the boats'll do, with us loaded deep with all kinds o' dynamite and stuff the like o' that! If a torpedo hits this hooker we'll all be in hell b'fore you could wink your eye.

JACK They ain't goin' to hit us, see? That's my dope. Whose wheel is it?

IVAN [*Sullenly*] My wheel. [*He lumbers out.*]

JACK And whose lookout?

SWANSON Mine, I tink. [*He follows* IVAN.]

JACK [*Scornfully*] A hell of a lot of use keepin' a lookout! We couldn't run away or fight if we wanted to. [*To* SCOTTY *and* SMITTY] Better look up the bo'sun or the Fourth, you two, and let 'em see you're awake. [SCOTTY *goes to the doorway and turns to wait for* SMITTY, *who is still in the same position, head on hands, seemingly unconscious of everything.* JACK *slaps him roughly on the shoulder and he comes to with a start.*] Aft and report, Duke! What's the matter with yuh—in a dope dream? [SMITTY *goes out after* SCOTTY *without answering.* JACK *looks after him with a frown.*] He's a queer guy. I can't figger him out.

DAVIS Nor no one else. [*Lowering his voice—meaningly*] An' he's liable to turn out queerer than any of us think if we ain't careful.

JACK [*Suspiciously*] What d'yuh mean? [*They are interrupted by the entrance of* DRISCOLL *and* COCKY.]

COCKY [*Protestingly*] Blimey if I don't fink I'll put in this 'ere watch ahtside on deck. [*He and* DRISCOLL *go over and get their cups.*] I down't want to be caught in this 'ole if they 'its us. [*He pours out coffee.*]

DRISCOLL [*Pouring his*] Divil a bit ut wud matther where ye arre. Ye'd be blown to smithereens b'fore ye cud say your name. [*He sits down, overturning as he does so the untouched cup of coffee which* SMITTY *had forgotten and left on the bench. They all jump nervously as the tin cup hits the floor with a bang.* DRISCOLL *flies into an unreasoning rage.*] Who's the dirty scut left this cup where a man 'ud sit on ut?

DAVIS It's Smitty's.

DRISCOLL [*Kicking the cup across the forecastle*] Does he think he's too much av a bloody gentleman to put his own away loike the rist av us? If he does I'm the bye'll beat that noshun out av his head.

COCKY Be the airs 'e puts on you'd think 'e was the Prince of Wales. Wot's 'e doin' on a ship, I arsks yer? 'E ain't now good as a sailor, is 'e?—dawdlin' abaht on deck like a chicken wiv 'is 'ead cut orf!

JACK [*Good-naturedly*] Aw, the Duke's all right. S'posin' he did ferget his cup—what's the dif? [*He picks up the cup and puts it away—with a grin.*] This war zone stuff's got yer goat, Drisc—and yours too, Cocky—and I ain't cheerin' much fur it myself, neither.

COCKY [*With a sigh*] Blimey, it ain't no bleedin' joke, yer first trip, to know as there's a ship full of shells li'ble to go orf in under your bloomin' feet, as you might say, if we gets 'it be a torpedo or mine. [*With sudden savagery*] Calls theyselves 'uman bein's, too! Blarsted 'Uns!

DRISCOLL [*Gloomily*] 'Tis me last trip in the bloody zone, God help me. The divil take their twenty-foive percent bonus—and be drowned like a rat in a trap in the bargain, maybe.

DAVIS Wouldn't be so bad if she wasn't carryin' ammunition. Them's the kind the subs is layin' for.

DRISCOLL [*Irritably*] Fur the love av hivin, don't be talkin' about ut. I'm sick wid thinkin' and jumpin' at iviry bit av a noise. [*There is a pause during which they all stare gloomily at the floor.*]

JACK Hey, Davis, what was you sayin' about Smitty when they come in?

DAVIS [*With a great air of mystery*]   I'll tell you in a minit. I want to wait an' see if he's comin' back. [*Impressively*] You won't be callin' him all right when you hears what I seen with my own eyes. [*He adds with an air of satisfaction*] An' you won't be feelin' no safer, neither. [*They all look at him with puzzled glances full of a vague apprehension.*]

DRISCOLL   God blarst ut! [*He fills his pipe and lights it. The others, with an air of remembering something they had forgotten, do the same.* SCOTTY *enters.*]

SCOTTY [*In awed tones*]   Mon, but it's clear outside the nicht! Like day.

DAVIS [*In low tones*]   Where's Smitty, Scotty?

SCOTTY   Out on the hatch starin' at the moon like a mon half-daft.

DAVIS   Kin you see him from the doorway?

SCOTTY [*Goes to doorway and carefully peeks out*] Aye; he's still there.

DAVIS   Keep your eyes on him for a moment. I've got something I wants to tell the boys and I don't want him walkin' in in the middle of it. Give a shout if he starts this way.

SCOTTY [*With suppressed excitement*]   Aye, I'll watch him. And I've somethin' myself to tell aboot his Lordship.

DRISCOLL [*Impatiently*]   Out wid ut! You're talkin' more than a pair av auld women wud be standin' in the road, and gittin' no further along.

DAVIS   Listen! You 'member when I went to git the coffee, Jack?

JACK   Sure, I do.

DAVIS Well, I brings it down here same as usual and got as far as the door there when I sees him.

JACK Smitty?

DAVIS Yes, Smitty! He was standin' in the middle of the fo'c's'le there [*Pointing*] lookin' around sneakin'-like at Ivan and Swanson and the rest 's if he wants to make certain they're asleep. [*He pauses significantly, looking from one to the other of his listeners.* SCOTTY *is nervously dividing his attention between* SMITTY *on the hatch outside and* DAVIS' *story, fairly bursting to break in with his own revelations.*]

JACK [*Impatiently*] What of it?

DAVIS Listen! He was standin' right there— [*Pointing again*] in his stockin' feet—no shoes on, mind, so he wouldn't make no noise!

JACK [*Spitting disgustedly*] Aw!

DAVIS [*Not heeding the interruption*] I seen right away somethin' on the queer was up so I slides back into the alleyway where I kin see him but he can't see me. After he makes sure they're all asleep he goes in under the bunks there—bein' careful not to raise a noise, mind!—an' takes out his bag there. [*By this time every one,* JACK *included, is listening breathlessly to his story.*] Then he fishes in his pocket an' takes out a bunch o' keys an' kneels down beside the bag an' opens it.

SCOTTY [*Unable to keep silent longer*] Mon, didn't I see him do that same thing wi' these two eyes. 'Twas just that moment I woke and spied him.

DAVIS [*Surprised, and a bit nettled to have to*

share his story with any one] Oh, you seen him, too, eh? [*To the others*] Then Scotty kin tell you if I'm lyin' or not.

DRISCOLL An' what did he do whin he'd the bag opened?

DAVIS He bends down and reaches out his hand sort o' scared-like, like it was somethin' dang'rous he was after, an' feels round in under his duds—hidden in under his duds an' wrapped up in 'em, it was— an' he brings out a black iron box!

COCKY [*Looking around him with a frightened glance*] Gawd blimey! [*The others likewise betray their uneasiness, shuffling their feet nervously.*]

DAVIS Ain't that right, Scotty?

SCOTTY Right as rain, I'm tellin' ye!

DAVIS [*To the others with an air of satisfaction*] There you are! [*Lowering his voice*] An' then what d'you suppose he did? Sneaks to his bunk an' slips the black box in under his mattress—in under his mattress, mind!

JACK And it's there now?

DAVIS Course it is! [JACK *starts toward* SMITTY'S *bunk.* DRISCOLL *grabs him by the arm.*]

DRISCOLL Don't be touchin' ut, JACK!

JACK Yuh needn't worry. I ain't goin' to touch it. [*He pulls up* SMITTY'S *mattress and looks down. The others stare at him, holding their breaths. He turns to them, trying hard to assume a careless tone.*] It's there, aw right.

COCKY [*Miserably upset*] I'm gointer 'op it aht on deck. [*He gets up but* DRISCOLL *pulls him down again.* COCKY *protests.*] It fair guvs me the trembles sittin' still in 'ere.

DRISCOLL [*Scornfully*] Are ye frightened, ye toad? 'Tis a hell av a thing fur grown men to be shiverin' loike children at a bit av a black box. [*Scratching his head in uneasy perplexity*] Still, ut's damn queer, the looks av ut.

DAVIS [*Sarcastically*] A bit of a black box, eh? How big d'you think them—[*He hesitates*]—things has to be—big as this fo'c's'le?

JACK [*In a voice meant to be reassuring*] Aw, hell! I'll bet it ain't nothin' but some coin he's saved he's got locked up in there.

DAVIS [*Scornfully*] That's likely, ain't it? Then why does he act so s'picious? He's been on ship near two year, ain't he? He knows damn well there ain't no thiefs in this fo'c's'le, don't he? An' you know 's well 's I do he didn't have no money when he came on board an' he ain't saved none since. Don't you? [JACK *doesn't answer.*] Listen! D'you know what he done after he put that thing in under his mattress?— an' Scotty'll tell you if I ain't speakin' truth. He looks round to see if any one's woke up——

SCOTTY I clapped my eyes shut when he turned round.

DAVIS An' then he crawls into his bunk an' shuts his eyes, an' starts in *snorin', pretendin'* he was asleep, mind!

SCOTTY Aye, I could hear him.

DAVIS An' when I goes to call him I don't even shake him. I just says, "Eight bells, Smitty," in

a'most a whisper-like, an' up he gets yawnin' an'
stretchin' fit to kill hisself 's if he'd been dead asleep.

COCKY   Gawd blimey!

DRISCOLL [*Shaking his head*]   Ut looks bad, divil
a doubt av ut.

DAVIS [*Excitedly*]   An' now I come to think of
it, there's the porthole. How'd it come to git open,
tell me that? I know'd well Paul never opened it.
Ain't he grumblin' about bein' cold all the time?

SCOTTY   The mon that opened it meant no good
to this ship, whoever he was.

JACK [*Sourly*]   What porthole? What're yuh
talkin' about?

DAVIS [*Pointing over* PAUL'S *bunk*]   There. It
was open when I come in. I felt the cold air on my
neck an' shut it. It would'a been clear 's a light-
house to any sub that was watchin'—an' we s'posed
to have all the ports blinded! Who'd do a dirty trick
like that? It wasn't none of us, nor Scotty here, nor
Swanson, nor Ivan. Who would it be, then?

COCKY [*Angrily*]   Must'a been 'is bloody Lordship.

DAVIS   For all's we know he might'a been signal-
lin' with it. They does it like that by winkin' a
light. Ain't you read how they gets caught doin' it
in London an' on the coast?

COCKY [*Firmly convinced now*]   An' wots 'e doin'
aht alone on the 'atch—keepin' 'isself clear of us
like 'e was afraid?

DRISCOLL   Kape your eye on him, Scotty.

SCOTTY   There's no a move oot o' him.

JACK [*In irritated perplexity*]   But, hell, ain't he an Englishman? What'd he wanta——

DAVIS   English? How d'we know he's English? Cos he talks it? That ain't no proof. Ain't you read in the papers how all them German spies they been catchin' in England has been livin' there for ten, often as not twenty years, an' talks English as good's any one? An' look here, ain't you noticed he don't talk natural? He talks it too damn good, that's what I mean. He don't talk exactly like a toff, does he, Cocky?

COCKY   Not like any toff as I ever met up wiv.

DAVIS   No; an' he don't talk it like us, that's certain. An' he don't look English. An' what d'we know about him when you come to look at it? Nothin'! He ain't ever said where he comes from or why. All we knows is he ships on here in London 'bout a year b'fore the war starts, as an A. B.—stole his papers most lik'ly—when he don't know how to box the compass, hardly. Ain't that queer in itself? An' was he ever open with us like a good shipmate? No; he's always had that sly air about him 's if he was hidin' somethin'.

DRISCOLL [*Slapping his thigh—angrily*]   Divil take me if I don't think ye have the truth av ut, Davis.

COCKY [*Scornfully*]   Lettin' on be 'is silly airs, and all, 'e's the son of a blarsted earl or somethink!

DAVIS   An' the name he calls hisself—Smith! I'd risk a quid of my next pay day that his real name is Schmidt, if the truth was known.

JACK [*Evidently fighting against his own conviction*] Aw, say, you guys give me a pain! What'd they want puttin' a spy on this old tub for?

DAVIS [*Shaking his head sagely*] They're deep ones, an' there's a lot o' things a sailor'll see in the ports he puts in ought to be useful to 'em. An' if he kin signal to 'em an' they blows us up it's one ship less, ain't it? [*Lowering his voice and indicating* SMITTY's *bunk*] Or if he blows us up hisself.

SCOTTY [*In alarmed tones*] Hush, mon! Here he comes! [SCOTTY *hurries over to a bench and sits down. A thick silence settles over the forecastle. The men look from one to another with uneasy glances.* SMITTY *enters and sits down beside his bunk. He is seemingly unaware of the dark glances of suspicion directed at him from all sides. He slides his hand back stealthily over his mattress and his fingers move, evidently feeling to make sure the box is still there. The others follow this movement carefully with quick looks out of the corners of their eyes. Their attitudes grow tense as if they were about to spring at him. Satisfied the box is safe,* SMITTY *draws his hand away slowly and utters a sigh of relief.*]

SMITTY [*In a casual tone which to them sounds sinister*] It's a good light night for the subs if there's any about. [*For a moment he sits staring in front of him. Finally he seems to sense the hostile atmosphere of the forecastle and looks from one to the other of the men in surprise. All of them avoid his eyes. He sighs with a puzzled expression and gets up and walks out of the doorway. There is silence*

*for a moment after his departure and then a storm
of excited talk breaks loose.*]

DAVIS Did you see him feelin' if it was there?

COCKY 'E ain't arf a sly one wiv 'is talk of submarines, Gawd blind 'im!

SCOTTY Did ve see the sneakin' looks he gave
us?

DRISCOLL If ivir I saw black shame on a man's
face 'twas on his whin he sat there!

JACK [*Thoroughly convinced at last*] He looked
bad to me. He's a crook, aw right.

DAVIS [*Excitedly*] What'll we do? We gotter do
somethin' quick or—— [*He is interrupted by the
sound of something hitting against the port side of
the forecastle with a dull, heavy thud. The men
start to their feet in wild-eyed terror and turn as if
they were going to rush for the deck. They stand
that way for a strained moment, scarcely breathing
and listening intently.*]

JACK [*With a sickly smile*] Hell! It's on'y a piece
of driftwood or a floatin' log. [*He sits down again.*]

DAVIS [*Sarcastically*] Or a mine that didn't go
off—that time—or a piece o' wreckage from some
ship they've sent to Davy Jones.

COCKY [*Mopping his brow with a trembling
hand*] Blimey! [*He sinks back weakly on a bench.*]

DRISCOLL [*Furiously*] God blarst ut! No man at
all cud be puttin' up wid the loike av this—an' I'm
not wan to be fearin' anything or any man in the
worrld'll stand up to me face to face; but this
divil's trickery in the darrk—— [*He starts for*

SMITTY's *bunk*.] I'll throw ut out wan av the portholes an' be done wid ut. [*He reaches toward the mattress*.]

SCOTTY [*Grabbing his arm—wildly*] Arre ye daft, mon?

DAVIS Don't monkey with it, Drisc. I knows what to do. Bring the bucket o' water here, Jack, will you? [JACK *gets it and brings it over to* DAVIS.] An' you, Scotty, see if he's back on the hatch.

SCOTTY [*Cautiously peering out*] Aye, he's sittin' there the noo.

DAVIS Sing out if he makes a move. Lift up the mattress, Drisc—careful now! [DRISCOLL *does so with infinite caution*.] Take it out, JACK—careful—don't shake it now, for Christ's sake! Here—put it in the water—easy! There, that's fixed it! [*They all sit down with great sighs of relief*.] The water'll git in and spoil it.

DRISCOLL [*Slapping* DAVIS *on the back*] Good wurrk for ye, Davis, ye scut! [*He spits on his hands aggressively*.] An' now what's to be done wid that black-hearted thraitor?

COCKY [*Belligerently*] Guv 'im a shove in the marf and 'eave 'im over the side!

DAVIS An' serve him right!

JACK Aw, say, give him a chance. Yuh can't prove nothin' till yuh find out what's in there.

DRISCOLL [*Heatedly*] Is ut more proof ye'd be needin' afther what we've seen an' heard? Then listen to me—an' ut's Driscoll talkin'—if there's divilmint in that box an' we see plain 'twas his plan to murrdher his own shipmates that have served him fair—— [*He raises his fist.*] I'll choke his rotten hearrt out wid me own hands, an' over the side wid him, and one man missin' in the mornin'.

DAVIS   An' no one the wiser. He's the balmy kind what commits suicide.

COCKY   They 'angs spies ashore.

JACK [*Resentfully*]   If he's done what yuh think I'll croak him myself. Is that good enough for yuh?

DRISCOLL [*Looking down at the box*]   How'll we be openin' this, I wonder?

SCOTTY [*From the doorway—warningly*]   He's standin' up.

DAVIS   We'll take his keys away from him when he comes in. Quick, Driscl You an' Jack get beside the door and grab him. [*They get on either side of the door. DAVIS snatches a small coil of rope from one of the upper bunks.*] This'll do for me an' Scotty to tie him.

SCOTTY   He's turrnin' this way—he's comin'! [*He moves away from door.*]

DAVIS   Stand by to lend a hand, Cocky.

COCKY   Righto. [*As SMITTY enters the forecastle he is seized roughly from both sides and his arms pinned behind him. At first he struggles fiercely, but seeing the uselessness of this, he finally stands calmly and allows DAVIS and SCOTTY to tie up his arms.*]

SMITTY [*When they have finished—with cold contempt*]   If this is your idea of a joke I'll have to confess it's a bit too thick for me to enjoy.

COCKY [*Angrily*]   Shut yer marf, 'ear!

DRISCOLL [*Roughly*]   Ye'll find ut's no joke, me bucko, b'fore we're done wid you. [*To SCOTTY*]

Kape your eye peeled, Scotty, and sing out if any one's comin'. [SCOTTY *resumes his post at the door.*]

SMITTY [*With the same icy contempt*] If you'd be good enough to explain——

DRISCOLL [*Furiously*] Explain, is ut? 'Tis you'll do the explainin'—an' damn quick, or we'll know the reason why. [*To* JACK *and* DAVIS] Bring him here, now. [*They push* SMITTY *over to the bucket.*] Look here, ye murrdherin' swab. D'you see ut? [SMITTY *looks down with an expression of amazement which rapidly changes to one of anguish.*]

DAVIS [*With a sneer*] Look at him! S'prised, ain't you? If you wants to try your dirty spyin' tricks on us you've gotter git up earlier in the mornin'.

COCKY Thorght yer weren't 'arf a fox, didn't yer?

SMITTY [*Trying to restrain his growing rage*] What—what do you mean? That's only—How dare— What are you doing with my private belongings?

COCKY [*Sarcastically*] Ho yus! Private b'longings!

DRISCOLL [*Shouting*] What is ut, ye swine? Will you tell us to our faces? What's in ut?

SMITTY [*Biting his lips—holding himself in check with a great effort*] Nothing but—— That's my business. You'll please attend to your own.

DRISCOLL Oho, ut is, is ut? [*Shaking his fist in* SMITTY's *face*] Talk aisy now if ye know what's best for you. Your business, indade! Then we'll be makin' ut ours, I'm thinkin'. [*To* JACK *and* DAVIS] Take his keys away from him an' we'll see if there's one'll open ut, maybe. [*They start in searching*

SMITTY, *who tries to resist and kicks out at the bucket.* DRISCOLL *leaps forward and helps them push him away.*] Try to kick ut over, wud ye? Did ye see him then? Tryin' to murrdher us all, the scut! Take that pail out av his way, Cocky. [SMITTY *struggles with all of his strength and keeps them busy for a few seconds. As* COCKY *grabs the pail* SMITTY *makes a final effort and, lunging forward, kicks again at the bucket but only succeeds in hitting* COCKY *on the shin.* COCKY *immediately sets down the pail with a bang and, clutching his knee in both hands, starts hopping around the forecastle, groaning and swearing.*]

COCKY Ooow! Gawd strike me pink! Kicked me, 'e did! Bloody, bleedin', rotten Dutch 'og! [*Approaching* SMITTY, *who has given up the fight and is pushed back against the wall near the doorway with* JACK *and* DAVIS *holding him on either side—wrathfully, at the top of his lungs*] Kick me, will yer? I'll show yer what for, yer bleedin' sneak! [*He draws back his fist.* DRISCOLL *pushes him to one side.*]

DRISCOLL Shut your mouth! D'you want to wake the whole ship? [COCKY *grumbles and retires to a bench, nursing his sore shin.*]

JACK [*Taking a small bunch of keys from* SMITTY'S *pocket*] Here yuh are, Drisc.

DRISCOLL [*Taking them*] We'll soon be knowin'. [*He takes the pail and sits down, placing it on the floor between his feet.* SMITTY *again tries to break loose but he is too tired and is easily held back against the wall.*]

SMITTY [*Breathing heavily and very pale*] Cowards!

JACK [*With a growl*] Nix on the rough talk, see! That don't git yuh nothin'.

DRISCOLL [*Looking at the lock on the box in the water and then scrutinizing the keys in his hand*] This'll be ut, I'm thinkin'. [*He selects one and gingerly reaches his hand in the water.*]

SMITTY [*His face grown livid—chokingly*] Don't you open that box, Driscoll. If you do, so help me God, I'll kill you if I have to hang for it.

DRISCOLL [*Pausing—his hand in the water*] Whin I open this box I'll not be the wan to be kilt, me sonny bye! I'm no dirty spy.

SMITTY [*His voice trembling with rage. His eyes are fixed on* DRISCOLL's *hand*] Spy? What are you talking about? I only put that box there so I could get it quick in case we were torpedoed. Are you all mad? Do you think I'm—— [*Chokingly*] You stupid curs! You cowardly dolts! [DAVIS *claps his hand over* SMITTY's *mouth.*]

DAVIS That'll be enough from you! [DRISCOLL *takes the dripping box from the water and starts to fit in the key.* SMITTY *springs forward furiously, almost escaping from their grasp, and drags them after him half-way across the forecastle.*]

DRISCOLL Hold him, ye divils! [*He puts the box back in the water and jumps to their aid.* COCKY *hovers on the outskirts of the battle, mindful of the kick he received.*]

SMITTY [*Raging*] Cowards! Damn you! Rotten

curs! [*He is thrown to the floor and held there.*] Cowards! Cowards!

DRISCOLL   I'll shut your dirty mouth for you. [*He goes to his bunk and pulls out a big wad of waste and comes back to* SMITTY.]

SMITTY   Cowards! Cowards!

DRISCOLL [*With no gentle hand slaps the waste over* SMITTY's *mouth*]   That'll teach you to be misnamin' a man, ye sneak. Have ye a handkerchief, Jack? [JACK *hands him one and he ties it tightly around* SMITTY's *head over the waste.*] That'll fix your gab. Stand him up, now, and tie his feet, too, so he'll not be movin'. [*They do so and leave him with his back against the wall near* SCOTTY. *Then they all sit down beside* DRISCOLL, *who again lifts the box out of the water and sets it carefully on his knees. He picks out the key, then hesitates, looking from one to the other uncertainly.*] We'd best be takin' this to the skipper, d'you think, maybe?

JACK [*Irritably*]   To hell with the Old Man. This is our game and we c'n play it without no help.

COCKY   Now bleedin' horficers, I says!

DAVIS   They'd only be takin' all the credit and makin' heroes of theyselves.

DRISCOLL [*Boldly*]   Here goes, thin! [*He slowly turns the key in the lock. The others instinctively turn away. He carefully pushes the cover back on its hinges and looks at what he sees inside with an expression of puzzled astonishment. The others crowd up close. Even* SCOTTY *leaves his post to take a look.*] What is ut, Davis?

DAVIS [*Mystified*]   Looks funny, don't it? Somethin' square tied up in a rubber bag. Maybe it's
dynamite—or somethin'—you can't never tell.

JACK   Aw, it ain't got no works so it ain't no
bomb, I'll bet.

DAVIS [*Dubiously*]   They makes them all kinds,
they do.

JACK   Open it up, Drisc.

DAVIS   Careful now! [DRISCOLL *takes a black
rubber bag resembling a large tobacco pouch from
the box and unties the string which is wound tightly
around the top. He opens it and takes out a small
packet of letters also tied up with string. He turns
these over in his hands and looks at the others
questioningly.*]

JACK [*With a broad grin*]   On'y letters! [*Slapping
DAVIS on the back*] Yuh're a hell of a Sherlock
Holmes, ain't yuh? Letters from his best girl too,
I'll bet. Let's turn the Duke loose, what d'yuh say?
[*He starts to get up.*]

DAVIS [*Fixing him with a withering look*]   Don't
be so damn smart, Jack. Letters, you says, 's if there
never was no harm in 'em. How d'you s'pose spies
gets their orders and sends back what they finds out
if it ain't by letters and such things? There's many
a letter is worser'n any bomb.

COCKY   Righto! They ain't as innercent as they
looks, I'll take me oath, when you read 'em. [*Pointing at SMITTY*] Not 'is Lordship's letters; not be no
means!

JACK [*Sitting down again*]   Well, read 'em and
find out. [DRISCOLL *commences untying the packet.*

There is a muffled groan of rage and protest from SMITTY.]

DAVIS [*Triumphantly*] There! Listen to him! Look at him tryin' to git loose! Ain't that proof enough? He knows well we're findin' him out. Listen to me! Love letters, you says, Jack, 's if they couldn't harm nothin'. Listen! I was readin' in some magazine in New York on'y two weeks back how some German spy in Paris was writin' love letters to some woman spy in Switzerland who sent 'em on to Berlin, Germany. To read 'em you wouldn't s'pect nothin'—just mush and all. [*Impressively*] But they had a way o' doin' it—a damn sneakin' way. They had a piece o' plain paper with pieces cut out of it an' when they puts it on top o' the letter they sees on'y the words what tells them what they wants to know. An' the Frenchies gets beat in a fight all on account o' that letter.

COCKY [*Awed*] Gawd blimey! They ain't 'arf smart bleeders!

DAVIS [*Seeing his audience is again all with him*] An' even if these letters of his do sound all right they may have what they calls a code. You can't never tell. [*To* DRISCOLL, *who has finished untying the packet.*] Read one of 'em, Drisc. My eyes is weak.

DRISCOLL [*Takes the first one out of its envelope and bends down to the lantern with it. He turns up the wick to give him a better light*] I'm no hand to be readin' but I'll try ut. [*Again there is a muffled groan from* SMITTY *as he strains at his bonds.*]

DAVIS [*Gloatingly*] Listen to him! He knows. Go ahead, Drisc!

DRISCOLL [*His brow furrowed with concentration*]
Ut begins: Dearest Man—— [*His eyes travel down
the page.*] An' thin there's a lot av blarney tellin'
him how much she misses him now she's gone away
to singin' school—an' how she hopes he'll settle
down to rale worrk an' not be skylarkin' around
now that she's away loike he used to before she met
up wid him—and ut ends: "I love you betther than
anythin' in the worrld. You know that, don't you,
dear? But b'fore I can agree to live out my life wid
you, you must prove to me that the black shadow—
I won't menshun uts hateful name but you know
what I mean—which might wreck both our lives,
does not exist for you. You can do that, can't you,
dear? Don't you see you must for my sake?" [*He
pauses for a moment—then adds gruffly.*] Uts signed:
"Edith." [*At the sound of the name* SMITTY, *who has
stood tensely with his eyes shut as if he were under-
going torture during the reading, makes a muffled
sound like a sob and half turns his face to the wall.*]

JACK [*Sympathetically*] Hell! What's the use of
readin' that stuff even if——

DAVIS [*Interrupting him sharply*]   Wait! Where's
that letter from, Drisc?

DRISCOLL   There's no address on the top av ut.

DAVIS [*Meaningly*]   What'd I tell you? Look at
the postmark, Drisc—on the envelope.

DRISCOLL   The name that's written is Sidney
Davidson, wan hundred an'——

DAVIS   Never mind that. O' course it's a false
name. Look at the postmark.

DRISCOLL   There's a furrin stamp on ut by the

looks av ut. The mark's blurred so it's hard to read. [*He spells it out laboriously.*] B-e-r—the nixt is an l, I think—i—an' an n.

DAVIS [*Excitedly*] Berlin! What did I tell you? I knew them letters was from Germany.

COCKY [*Shaking his fist in* SMITTY's *direction*] Rotten 'ound! [*The others look at* SMITTY *as if this last fact had utterly condemned him in their eyes.*]

DAVIS Give me the letter, Drisc. Maybe I kin make somethin' out of it. [DRISCOLL *hands the letter to him.*] You go through the others, Drisc, and sing out if you sees anythin' queer. [*He bends over the first letter as if he were determined to figure out its secret meaning.* JACK, COCKY *and* SCOTTY *look over his shoulder with eager curiosity.* DRISCOLL *takes out some of the other letters, running his eyes quickly down the pages. He looks curiously over at* SMITTY *from time to time, and sighs frequently with a puzzled frown.*]

DAVIS [*Disappointedly*] I gotter give it up. It's too deep for me, but we'll turn 'em over to the perlice when we docks at Liverpool to look through. This one I got was written a year before the war started, anyway. Find anythin' in yours, Drisc?

DRISCOLL They're all the same as the first—lovin' blarney, an' how her singin' is doin', and the great things the Dutch teacher says about her voice, an' how glad she is that her Sidney bye is worrkin' harrd an' makin' a man av himself for her sake. [SMITTY *turns his face completely to the wall.*]

DAVIS [*Disgustedly*] If we on'y had the code!

DRISCOLL [*Taking up the bottom letter*] Hullo!

Here's wan addressed to this ship—s. s. *Glencairn,* ut
says—whin we was in Cape Town sivin months
ago—— [*Looking at the postmark*] Ut's from London.

DAVIS [*Eagerly*] Read it! [*There is another
choking groan from* SMITTY.]

DRISCOLL [*Reads slowly—his voice becomes lower
and lower as he goes on*]   Ut begins wid simply the
name Sidney Davidson—no dearest or sweetheart to
this wan. "Ut is only from your chance meetin' wid
Harry—whin you were drunk—that I happen to
know where to reach you. So you have run away
to sea loike the coward you are because you knew
I had found out the truth—the truth you have
covered over with your mean little lies all the time
I was away in Berlin and blindly trusted you. Very
well, you have chosen. You have shown that your
drunkenness means more to you than any love or
faith av mine. I am sorry—for I loved you, Sidney
Davidson—but this is the end. I lave you—the
mem'ries; an' if ut is any satisfaction to you I lave
you the real-i-zation that you have wrecked my loife
as you have wrecked your own. My one remainin'
hope is that nivir in God's worrld will I ivir see
your face again. Goodby. Edith." [*As he finishes
there is a deep silence, broken only by* SMITTY'S
*muffled sobbing. The men cannot look at each
other.* DRISCOLL *holds the rubber bag limply in his
hand and some small white object falls out of it and
drops noiselessly on the floor. Mechanically* DRIS-
COLL *leans over and picks it up, and looks at it wonderingly.*]

DAVIS [*In a dull voice*] What's that?

DRISCOLL [*Slowly*] A bit av a dried-up flower,—a rose, maybe. [*He drops it into the bag and gathers up the letters and puts them back. He replaces the bag in the box, and locks it and puts it back under* SMITTY's *mattress. The others follow him with their eyes. He steps softly over to* SMITTY *and cuts the ropes about his arms and ankles with his sheath knife, and unties the handkerchief over the gag.* SMITTY *does not turn around but covers his face with his hands and leans his head against the wall. His shoulders continue to heave spasmodically but he makes no further sound.*]

DRISCOLL [*Stalks back to the others—there is a moment of silence, in which each man is in agony with the hopelessness of finding a word he can say— then* DRISCOLL *explodes*] God stiffen us, are we never goin' to turn in fur a wink av sleep? [*They all start as if awakening from a bad dream and gratefully crawl into their bunks, shoes and all, turning their faces to the wall, and pulling their blankets up over their shoulders.* SCOTTY *tiptoes past* SMITTY *out into the darkness . . .* DRISCOLL *turns down the light and crawls into his bunk as*

[*The curtain falls.*]

ILE

A Play in One Act

CHARACTERS

BEN, *the cabin boy*
THE STEWARD
CAPTAIN KEENEY
SLOCUM, *second mate*
MRS. KEENEY
JOE, *a harpooner*
Members of the crew
    of the steam whaler Atlantic Queen

ILE

SCENE CAPTAIN KEENEY's *cabin on board the steam whaling ship* Atlantic Queen—*a small, square compartment about eight feet high with a skylight in the center looking out on the poop deck. On the left (the stern of the ship) a long bench with rough cushions is built in against the wall. In front of the bench, a table. Over the bench, several curtained portholes.*

In the rear, left, a door leading to the captain's sleeping quarters. To the right of the door a small organ, looking as if it were brand new, is placed against the wall.

On the right, to the rear, a marble-topped sideboard. On the sideboard, a woman's sewing basket. Farther forward, a doorway leading to the companionway, and past the officers' quarters to the main deck.

In the center of the room, a stove. From the middle of the ceiling a hanging lamp is suspended. The walls of the cabin are painted white.

There is no rolling of the ship, and the light which comes through the skylight is

*sickly and faint, indicating one of those gray
days of calm when ocean and sky are alike
dead. The silence is unbroken except for the
measured tread of some one walking up and
down on the poop deck overhead.*

*It is nearing two bells—one o'clock—in the
afternoon of a day in the year 1895.*

*At the rise of the curtain there is a moment
of intense silence. Then the* STEWARD *enters
and commences to clear the table of the few
dishes which still remain on it after the* CAP-
TAIN's *dinner. He is an old, grizzled man
dressed in dungaree pants, a sweater, and a
woolen cap with ear flaps. His manner is
sullen and angry. He stops stacking up the
plates and casts a quick glance upward at
the skylight; then tiptoes over to the closed
door in rear and listens with his ear pressed
to the crack. What he hears makes his face
darken and he mutters a furious curse. There
is a noise from the doorway on the right and
he darts back to the table.*

*BEN enters. He is an over-grown, gawky
boy with a long, pinched face. He is dressed
in sweater, fur cap, etc. His teeth are chattering with the cold and he hurries to the stove,
where he stands for a moment shivering,
blowing on his hands, slapping them against
his sides, on the verge of crying.*

THE STEWARD [*In relieved tones—seeing who it
is*]   Oh, 'tis you, is it? What're ye shiverin' 'bout?

Stay by the stove where ye belong and ye'll find no need of chatterin'.

BEN It's c-c-cold. [*Trying to control his chattering teeth—derisively*] Who d'ye think it were—the Old Man?

THE STEWARD [*Makes a threatening move—*BEN *shrinks away*] None o' your lip, young un, or I'll learn ye. [*More kindly*] Where was it ye've been all o' the time—the fo'c's'le?

BEN Yes.

THE STEWARD Let the Old Man see ye up for'ard monkeyshinin' with the hands and ye'll get a hidin' ye'll not forget in a hurry.

BEN Aw, he don't see nothin'. [*A trace of awe in his tones—he glances upward.*] He just walks up and down like he didn't notice nobody—and stares at the ice to the no'th'ard.

THE STEWARD [*The same tone of awe creeping into his voice*] He's always starin' at the ice. [*In a sudden rage, shaking his fist at the skylight*] Ice, ice, ice! Damn him and damn the ice! Holdin' us in for nigh on a year—nothin' to see but ice—stuck in it like a fly in molasses!

BEN [*Apprehensively*] Ssshh! He'll hear ye.

THE STEWARD [*Raging*] Aye, damn him, and damn the Arctic seas, and damn this stinkin' whalin' ship of his, and damn me for a fool to ever ship on it! [*Subsiding as if realizing the uselessness of this outburst—shaking his head—slowly, with deep conviction*] He's a hard man—as hard a man as ever sailed the seas.

BEN [*Solemnly*] Aye.

THE STEWARD   The two years we all signed up
for are done this day. Blessed Christ! Two years o'
this dog's life, and no luck in the fishin', and the
hands half starved with the food runnin' low, rotten
as it is; and not a sign of him turnin' back for
home! [*Bitterly*] Home! I begin to doubt if ever
I'll set foot on land again. [*Excitedly*] What is it he
thinks he's goin' to do? Keep us all up here after our
time is worked out till the last man of us is starved
to death or frozen? We've grub enough hardly to
last out the voyage back if we started now. What
are the men goin' to do 'bout it? Did ye hear any
talk in the fo'c's'le?

BEN [*Going over to him—in a half whisper*]
They said if he don't put back south for home to-
day they're goin' to mutiny.

THE STEWARD [*With grim satisfaction*]   Mutiny?
Aye, 'tis the only thing they can do; and serve him
right after the manner he's treated them—'s if they
wern't no better nor dogs.

BEN   The ice is all broke up to s'uth'ard. They's
clear water 's far 's you can see. He ain't got no
excuse for not turnin' back for home, the men says.

THE STEWARD [*Bitterly*]   He won't look no-
wheres but no'th'ard where they's only the ice to
see. He don't want to see no clear water. All he
thinks on is gittin' the ile—'s if it was our fault he
ain't had good luck with the whales. [*Shaking his
head*] I think the man's mighty nigh losin' his
senses.

BEN [*Awed*]   D'you really think he's crazy?

THE STEWARD   Aye, it's the punishment o' God

on him. Did ye ever hear of a man who wasn't crazy do the things he does? [*Pointing to the door in rear*] Who but a man that's mad would take his woman—and as sweet a woman as ever was—on a stinkin' whalin' ship to the Arctic seas to be locked in by the rotten ice for nigh on a year, and maybe lose her senses forever—for it's sure she'll never be the same again.

BEN [*Sadly*] She useter be awful nice to me before—— [*His eyes grow wide and frightened*] she got—like she is.

THE STEWARD Aye, she was good to all of us. 'Twould have been hell on board without her, for he's a hard man—a hard, hard man—a driver if there ever was one. [*With a grim laugh*] I hope he's satisfied now—drivin' her on till she's near lost her mind. And who could blame her? 'Tis a God's wonder we're not a ship full of crazed people—with the damned ice all the time, and the quiet so thick you're afraid to hear your own voice.

BEN [*With a frightened glance toward the door on right*] She don't never speak to me no more—jest looks at me 's if she didn't know me.

THE STEWARD She don't know no one—but him. She talks to him—when she does talk—right enough.

BEN She does nothin' all day long now but sit and sew—and then she cries to herself without makin' no noise. I've seen her.

THE STEWARD Aye, I could hear her through the door a while back.

BEN [*Tiptoes over to the door and listens*] She's cryin' now.

THE STEWARD [*Furiously—shaking his fist*] God send his soul to hell for the devil he is! [*There is the noise of some one coming slowly down the companionway stairs.* THE STEWARD *hurries to his stacked-up dishes. He is so nervous from fright that he knocks off the top one, which falls and breaks on the floor. He stands aghast, trembling with dread.* BEN *is violently rubbing off the organ with a piece of cloth which he has snatched from his pocket.* CAPTAIN KEENEY *appears in the doorway on right and comes into the cabin, removing his fur cap as he does so. He is a man of about forty, around five-ten in height but looking much shorter on account of the enormous proportions of his shoulders and chest. His face is massive and deeply lined, with gray-blue eyes of a bleak hardness, and a tightly clenched, thin-lipped mouth. His thick hair is long and gray. He is dressed in a heavy blue jacket and blue pants stuffed into his seaboots.*

[*He is followed into the cabin by the* SECOND MATE, *a rangy six-footer with a lean weatherbeaten face. The* MATE *is dressed about the same as the captain. He is a man of thirty or so.*]

KEENEY [*Comes toward the* STEWARD—*with a stern look on his face. The* STEWARD *is visibly frightened and the stack of dishes rattles in his trembling hands.* KEENEY *draws back his fist and the* STEWARD *shrinks away. The fist is gradually lowered and* KEENEY *speaks slowly*] 'Twould be like hitting a worm. It is nigh on two bells, Mr. Steward, and this truck not cleared yet.

THE STEWARD [*Stammering*] Y-y-yes, sir.

KEENEY Instead of doin' your rightful work
ye've been below here gossipin' old woman's talk
with that boy. [*To* BEN, *fiercely*] Get out o' this,
you! Clean up the chart room. [BEN *darts past the*
MATE *to the open doorway.*] Pick up that dish,
MR. STEWARD!

THE STEWARD [*Doing so with difficulty*] Yes, sir.

KEENEY The next dish you break, Mr. Steward,
you take a bath in the Bering Sea at the end of a
rope.

THE STEWARD [*Tremblingly*] Yes, sir. [*He
hurries out. The* SECOND MATE *walks slowly over to
the* CAPTAIN.]

MATE I warn't 'specially anxious the man at
the wheel should catch what I wanted to say to you,
sir. That's why I asked you to come below.

KEENEY [*Impatiently*] Speak your say, Mr.
Slocum.

MATE [*Unconsciously lowering his voice*] I'm
afeard there'll be trouble with the hands by the
look o' things. They'll likely turn ugly, every
blessed one o' them, if you don't put back. The
two years they signed up for is up to-day.

KEENEY And d'you think you're tellin' me
somethin' new, Mr. Slocum? I've felt it in the air this
long time past. D'you think I've not seen their ugly
looks and the grudgin' way they worked? [*The door
in rear is opened and* MRS. KEENEY *stands in the
doorway. She is a slight, sweet-faced little woman
primly dressed in black. Her eyes are red from
weeping and her face drawn and pale. She takes in
the cabin with a frightened glance and stands as if*

*fixed to the spot by some nameless dread, clasping
and unclasping her hands nervously. The two men
turn and look at her.*]

KEENEY [*With rough tenderness*] Well, Annie?

MRS. KEENEY [*As if awakening from a dream*]
David, I—— [*She is silent. The* MATE *starts for the
doorway.*]

KEENEY [*Turning to him—sharply*] Wait!

MATE Yes, sir.

KEENEY D'you want anything, Annie?

MRS. KEENEY [*After a pause, during which she
seems to be endeavoring to collect her thoughts*] I
thought maybe—I'd go up on deck, David, to get
a breath of fresh air. [*She stands humbly awaiting
his permission. He and the* MATE *exchange a significant glance.*]

KEENEY It's too cold, Annie. You'd best stay
below to-day. There's nothing to look at on deck—
but ice.

MRS. KEENEY [*Monotonously*] I know—ice, ice,
ice! But there's nothing to see down here but these
walls. [*She makes a gesture of loathing.*]

KEENEY You can play the organ, Annie.

MRS. KEENEY [*Dully*] I hate the organ. It puts
me in mind of home.

KEENEY [*A touch of resentment in his voice*] I
got it jest for you.

MRS. KEENEY [*Dully*] I know. [*She turns away
from them and walks slowly to the bench on left.
She lifts up one of the curtains and looks through a
porthole; then utters an exclamation of joy.*] Ah,

water! Clear water! As far as I can see! How good it looks after all these months of ice! [*She turns round to them, her face transfigured with joy.*] Ah, now I must go upon deck and look at it, David.

KEENEY [*Frowning*] Best not to-day, Annie. Best wait for a day when the sun shines.

MRS. KEENEY [*Desperately*] But the sun never shines in this terrible place.

KEENEY [*A tone of command in his voice*] Best not to-day, Annie.

MRS. KEENEY (*Crumbling before this command— abjectly*] Very well, David. [*She stands there staring straight before her as if in a daze. The two men look at her uneasily.*]

KEENEY [*Sharply*] Annie!

MRS. KEENEY [*Dully*] Yes, David.

KEENEY Me and Mr. Slocum has business to talk about—ship's business.

MRS. KEENEY Very well, David. [*She goes slowly out, rear, and leaves the door three-quarters shut behind her.*]

KEENEY Best not have her on deck if they's goin' to be any trouble.

MATE Yes, sir.

KEENEY And trouble they's goin' to be. I feel it in my bones. [*Takes a revolver from the pocket of his coat and examines it.*] Got your'n?

MATE Yes, sir.

KEENEY Not that we'll have to use 'em—not if I know their breed of dog—jest to frighten 'em up a bit. [*Grimly*] I ain't never been forced to use one

yit; and trouble I've had by land and by sea 's long
as I kin remember, and will have till my dyin'
day, I reckon.

MATE [*Hesitatingly*] Then you ain't goin'—to
turn back?

KEENEY Turn back! Mr. Slocum, did you ever
hear 'o me pointin' s'uth for home with only a
measly four hundred barrel of ile in the hold?

MATE [*Hastily*] No, sir—but the grub's gittin'
low.

KEENEY They's enough to last a long time yit, if
they're careful with it; and they's plenty o' water.

MATE They say it's not fit to eat—what's left;
and the two years they signed on fur is up to-day.
They might make trouble for you in the courts
when we git home.

KEENEY To hell with 'em! Let them make what
law trouble they kin. I don't give a damn 'bout
the money. I've got to git the ile! [*Glancing sharply
at the* MATE] You ain't turnin' no damned sea
lawyer, be you, Mr. Slocum?

MATE [*Flushing*] Not by a hell of a sight, sir.

KEENEY What do the fools want to go home fur
now? Their share o' the four hundred barrel
wouldn't keep 'em in chewin' terbacco.

MATE [*Slowly*] They wants to git back to their
folks an' things, I s'pose.

KEENEY [*Looking at him searchingly*] 'N' you
want to turn back, too. [THE MATE *looks down confusedly before his sharp gaze.*] Don't lie, Mr. Slocum.
It's writ down plain in your eyes. [*With grim sar-*

casm] I hope, Mr. Slocum, you ain't agoin' to jine the men agin me.

MATE [*Indignantly*]   That ain't fair, sir, to say sich things.

KEENEY [*With satisfaction*]   I warn't much afeard o' that, Tom. You been with me nigh on ten year and I've learned ye whalin'. No man kin say I ain't a good master, if I be a hard one.

MATE   I warn't thinkin' of myself, sir—'bout turnin' home, I mean. [*Desperately*] But Mrs. Keeney, sir—seems like she ain't jest satisfied up here, ailin' like—what with the cold an' bad luck an' the ice an' all.

KEENEY [*His face clouding—rebukingly but not severely*]   That's my business, Mr. Slocum. I'll thank you to steer a clear course o' that. [*A pause*] The ice'll break up soon to no'th'ard. I could see it startin' to-day. And when it goes and we git some sun Annie'll perk up. [*Another pause—then he bursts forth*] It ain't the damned money what's keepin' me up in the Northern seas, Tom. But I can't go back to Homeport with a measly four hundred barrel of ile. I'd die fust. I ain't never come back home in all my days without a full ship. Ain't that truth?

MATE   Yes, sir; but this voyage you been ice-bound, an'——

KEENEY [*Scornfully*]   And d'you s'pose any of 'em would believe that—any o' them skippers I've beaten voyage after voyage? Can't you hear 'em laughin' and sneerin'—Tibbots 'n' Harris 'n' Simms and the rest—and all o' Homeport makin' fun o' me? "Dave Keeney what boasts he's the best whalin' skipper out o' Homeport comin' back with a measly four hundred barrel of ile?" [*The thought of this drives him into a frenzy, and he smashes his fist down on the marble top of the sideboard.*] Hell! I got to git the ile, I tell you. How could I figger on this ice? It's never been so bad before in the thirty year I been acomin' here. And now it's breakin' up. In a couple o' days it'll be all gone. And they's whale here, plenty of 'em. I know they is and I ain't never gone wrong yit. I got to git the ile! I got to git it in spite of all hell, and by God, I ain't agoin' home till I do git it! [*There is the sound of subdued sobbing from the door in rear. The two men stand silent for a moment, listening. Then* KEENEY *goes over to the door and looks in. He hesitates for a moment as if he were going to enter—then closes the door softly.* JOE, *the harpooner, an enormous six-footer with a battered, ugly face, enters from right and stands waiting for the captain to notice him.*]

KEENEY [*Turning and seeing him*] Don't be standin' there like a gawk, Harpooner. Speak up!

JOE [*Confusedly*] We want—the men, sir—they wants to send a depitation aft to have a word with you.

KEENEY [*Furiously*] Tell 'em to go to——[*Checks himself and continues grimly*] Tell 'em to come. I'll see 'em.

JOE Aye, aye, sir. [*He goes out.*]

KEENEY [*With a grim smile*] Here it comes, the trouble you spoke of, Mr. Slocum, and we'll make short shift of it. It's better to crush such things at the start than let them make headway.

MATE [*Worriedly*] Shall I wake up the First and Fourth, sir? We might need their help.

KEENEY No, let them sleep. I'm well able to handle this alone, Mr. Slocum. [*There is the shuffling of footsteps from outside and five of the crew crowd into the cabin, led by* JOE. *All are dressed alike—sweaters, seaboots, etc. They glance uneasily at the* CAPTAIN, *twirling their fur caps in their hands.*]

KEENEY [*After a pause*] Well? Who's to speak fur ye?

JOE [*Stepping forward with an air of bravado*] I be.

KEENEY [*Eyeing him up and down coldly*] So you be. Then speak your say and be quick about it.

JOE [*Trying not to wilt before the* CAPTAIN's *glance and avoiding his eyes*] The time we signed up for is done to-day.

KEENEY [*Icily*] You're tellin' me nothin' I don't know.

JOE You ain't pintin' fur home yit, far 's we kin see.

KEENEY No, and I ain't agoin' to till this ship is full of ile.

JOE You can't go no further no'th with the ice afore ye.

KEENEY The ice is breaking up.

JOE [*After a slight pause during which the others mumble angrily to one another*] The grub we're gittin' now is rotten.

KEENEY It's good enough fur ye. Better men than ye are have eaten worse. [*There is a chorus of angry exclamations from the crowd.*]

JOE [*Encouraged by this support*] We ain't agoin' to work no more less you puts back for home.

KEENEY [*Fiercely*] You ain't, ain't you?

JOE No; and the law courts'll say we was right.

KEENEY To hell with your law courts! We're at sea now and I'm the law on this ship. [*Edging up toward the harpooner*] And every mother's son of you what don't obey orders goes in irons. [*There are more angry exclamations from the crew. MRS. KEENEY appears in the doorway in rear and looks on with startled eyes. None of the men notice her.*]

JOE [*With bravado*] Then we're agoin' to mutiny and take the old hooker home ourselves. Ain't we, boys? [*As he turns his head to look at the others, KEENEY's fist shoots out to the side of his jaw. JOE goes down in a heap and lies there. MRS. KEENEY gives a shriek and hides her face in her hands. The men pull out their sheath knives and start a rush, but stop when they find themselves confronted by the revolvers of KEENEY and the MATE.*]

KEENEY [*His eyes and voice snapping*] Hold still! [*The men stand huddled together in a sullen silence. KEENEY's voice is full of mockery.*] You've found out it ain't safe to mutiny on this ship, ain't you? And now git for'ard where ye belong, and——

[*He gives* JOE's *body a contemptuous kick.*] Drag him with you. And remember the first man of ye I see shirkin' I'll shoot dead as sure as there's a sea under us, and you can tell the rest the same. Git for'ard now! Quick! [*The men leave in cowed silence, carrying* JOE *with them.* KEENEY *turns to the* MATE *with a short laugh and puts his revolver back in his pocket.*] Best get up on deck, Mr. Slocum, and see to it they don't try none of their skulkin' tricks. We'll have to keep an eye peeled from now on. I know 'em.

MATE Yes, sir. [*He goes out, right.* KEENEY *hears his wife's hysterical weeping and turns around in surprise—then walks slowly to her side.*]

KEENEY [*Putting an arm around her shoulder—with gruff tenderness*] There, there, Annie. Don't be afeard. It's all past and gone.

MRS. KEENEY [*Shrinking away from him*] Oh, I can't bear it! I can't bear it any longer!

KEENEY [*Gently*] Can't bear what, Annie?

MRS. KEENEY [*Hysterically*] All this horrible brutality, and these brutes of men, and this terrible ship, and this prison cell of a room, and the ice all around, and the silence. [*After this outburst she calms down and wipes her eyes with her handkerchief.*]

KEENEY [*After a pause during which he looks down at her with a puzzled frown*] Remember, I warn't hankerin' to have you come on this voyage, Annie.

MRS. KEENEY I wanted to be with you, David, don't you see? I didn't want to wait back there in the house all alone as I've been doing these last six years since we were married—waiting, and watching, and fearing—with nothing to keep my mind occupied—not able to go back teaching school on account of being Dave Keeney's wife. I used to dream of sailing on the great, wide, glorious ocean. I wanted to be by your side in the danger and vigorous life of it all. I wanted to see you the hero they make you out to be in Homeport. And instead—— [*Her voice grows tremulous.*] All I find is ice and cold—and brutality! [*Her voice breaks.*]

KEENEY   I warned you what it'd be, Annie. "Whalin' ain't no ladies' tea party," I says to you, and "You better stay to home where you've got all your woman's comforts." [*Shaking his head*] But you was so set on it.

MRS. KEENEY [*Wearily*]   Oh, I know it isn't your fault, David. You see, I didn't believe you. I guess I was dreaming about the old Vikings in the story books and I thought you were one of them.

KEENEY [*Protestingly*]   I done my best to make it as cozy and comfortable as could be. [MRS. KEENEY *looks around her in wild scorn.*] I even sent to the city for that organ for ye, thinkin' it might be soothin' to ye to be playin' it times when they was calms and things was dull like.

MRS. KEENEY [*Wearily*]   Yes, you were very kind, David. I know that. [*She goes to left and lifts the curtains from the porthole and looks out—then suddenly bursts forth*] I won't stand it—I can't stand it—pent up by these walls like a prisoner. [*She runs over to him and throws her arms around him, weeping. He puts his arm protectingly over her shoulders.*] Take me away from here, David! If I don't get away from here, out of this terrible ship, I'll go mad! Take me home, David! I can't think any more. I feel as if the cold and the silence were crushing down on my brain. I'm afraid. Take me home!

KEENEY [*Holds her at arm's length and looks at her face anxiously*] Best go to bed, Annie. You ain't yourself. You got fever. Your eyes look so strange like. I ain't never seen you look this way before.

MRS. KEENEY [*Laughing hysterically*] It's the ice and the cold and the silence—they'd make any one look strange.

KEENEY [*Soothingly*] In a month or two, with good luck, three at the most, I'll have her filled with ile and then we'll give her everything she'll stand and pint for home.

MRS. KEENEY But we can't wait for that—I can't wait. I want to get home. And the men won't wait. They want to get home. It's cruel, it's brutal for you to keep them. You must sail back. You've got no excuse. There's clear water to the south now. If you've a heart at all you've got to turn back.

KEENEY [*Harshly*] I can't, Annie.

MRS. KEENEY Why can't you?

KEENEY A woman couldn't rightly understand my reason.

MRS. KEENEY [*Wildly*] Because it's a stupid, stubborn reason. Oh, I heard you talking with the second mate. You're afraid the other captains will

sneer at you because you didn't come back with a
full ship. You want to live up to your silly reputa-
tion even if you do have to beat and starve men
and drive me mad to do it.

KEENEY [*His jaw set stubbornly*] It ain't that,
Annie. Them skippers would never dare sneer to
my face. It ain't so much what any one'd say—
but—— [*He hesitates, struggling to express his meaning.*] You see—I've always done it—since my first
voyage as skipper. I always come back—with a full
ship—and—it don't seem right not to—somehow. I
been always first whalin' skipper out o' Homeport,
and—— Don't you see my meanin', Annie? [*He
glances at her. She is not looking at him but staring
dully in front of her, not hearing a word he is saying.*] Annie! [*She comes to herself with a start.*] Best
turn in, Annie, there's a good woman. You ain't
well.

MRS. KEENEY [*Resisting his attempts to guide her
to the door in rear*] David! Won't you please turn
back?

KEENEY [*Gently*] I can't, Annie—not yet awhile.
You don't see my meanin'. I got to git the ile.

MRS. KEENEY It'd be different if you needed the
money, but you don't. You've got more than plenty.

KEENEY [*Impatiently*] It ain't the money I'm
thinkin' of. D'you think I'm as mean as that?

MRS. KEENEY [*Dully*] No—I don't know—I can't
understand—— [*Intensely*] Oh, I want to be home in
the old house once more and see my own kitchen
again, and hear a woman's voice talking to me and
be able to talk to her. Two years! It seems so long

ago—as if I'd been dead and could never go back.

KEENEY [*Worried by her strange tone and the far-away look in her eyes*] Best go to bed, Annie. You ain't well.

MRS. KEENEY [*Not appearing to hear him*] I used to be lonely when you were away. I used to think Homeport was a stupid, monotonous place. Then I used to go down on the beach, especially when it was windy and the breakers were rolling in, and I'd dream of the fine free life you must be leading. [*She gives a laugh which is half a sob.*] I used to love the sea then. [*She pauses; then continues with slow intensity*] But now—I don't ever want to see the sea again.

KEENEY [*Thinking to humor her*] 'Tis no fit place for a woman, that's sure. I was a fool to bring ye.

MRS. KEENEY [*After a pause—passing her hand over her eyes with a gesture of pathetic weariness*] How long would it take us to reach home—if we started now?

KEENEY [*Frowning*] 'Bout two months, I reckon, Annie, with fair luck.

MRS. KEENEY [*Counts on her fingers—then murmurs with a rapt smile*] That would be August, the latter part of August, wouldn't it? It was on the twenty-fifth of August we were married, David, wasn't it?

KEENEY [*Trying to conceal the fact that her memories have moved him—gruffly*] Don't you remember?

MRS. KEENEY [*Vaguely—again passes her hand*

over her eyes] My memory is leaving me—up here in the ice. It was so long ago. [*A pause—then she smiles dreamily.*] It's June now. The lilacs will be all in bloom in the front yard—and the climbing roses on the trellis to the side of the house—they're budding. [*She suddenly covers her face with her hands and commences to sob.*]

KEENEY [*Disturbed*] Go in and rest, Annie. You're all wore out cryin' over what can't be helped.

MRS. KEENEY [*Suddenly throwing her arms around his neck and clinging to him*] You love me, don't you, David?

KEENEY [*In amazed embarrassment at this outburst*] Love you? Why d'you ask me such a question, Annie?

MRS. KEENEY [*Shaking him—fiercely*] But you do, don't you, David? Tell me!

KEENEY I'm your husband, Annie, and you're my wife. Could there be aught but love between us after all these years?

MRS. KEENEY [*Shaking him again—still more fiercely*] Then you do love me. Say it!

KEENEY [*Simply*] I do, Annie.

MRS. KEENEY [*Gives a sigh of relief—her hands drop to her sides. Keeney regards her anxiously. She passes her hand across her eyes and murmurs half to herself*] I sometimes think if we could only have had a child. [KEENEY *turns away from her, deeply moved. She grabs his arm and turns him around to face her—intensely.*] And I've always been a good wife to you, haven't I, David?

KEENEY [*His voice betraying his emotion*] No man has ever had a better, Annie.

MRS. KEENEY And I've never asked for much from you, have I, David? Have I?

KEENEY You know you could have all I got the power to give ye, Annie.

MRS. KEENEY [*Wildly*] Then do this this once for my sake, for God's sake—take me home! It's killing me, this life—the brutality and cold and horror of it. I'm going mad. I can feel the threat in the air. I can hear the silence threatening me—day after gray day and every day the same. I can't bear it. [*Sobbing*] I'll go mad, I know I will. Take me home, David, if you love me as you say. I'm afraid. For the love of God, take me home! [*She throws her arms around him, weeping against his shoulder. His face betrays the tremendous struggle going on within him. He holds her out at arm's length, his expression softening. For a moment his shoulders sag, he becomes old, his iron spirit weakens as he looks at her tear-stained face.*]

KEENEY [*Dragging out the words with an effort*] I'll do it, Annie—for your sake—if you say it's needful for ye.

MRS. KEENEY [*With wild joy—kissing him*] God bless you for that, David! [*He turns away from her silently and walks toward the companionway. Just at that moment there is a clatter of footsteps on the stairs and the* SECOND MATE *enters the cabin.*]

MATE [*Excitedly*] The ice is breakin' up to no'th'ard, sir. There's a clear passage through the floe, and clear water beyond, the lookout says.

[KEENEY *straightens himself like a man coming out of a trance.* MRS. KEENEY *looks at the* MATE *with terrified eyes.*]

KEENEY [*Dazedly—trying to collect his thoughts*] A clear passage? To no'th'ard?

MATE   Yes, sir.

KEENEY [*His voice suddenly grim with determination*]   Then get her ready and we'll drive her through.

MATE   Aye, aye, sir.

MRS. KEENEY [*Appealingly*]   David!

KEENEY [*Not heeding her*]   Will the men turn to willin' or must we drag 'em out?

MATE   They'll turn to willin' enough. You put the fear o' God into 'em, sir. They're meek as lambs.

KEENEY   Then drive 'em—both watches. [*With grim determination*]   They's whale t'other side o' this floe and we're going to git 'em.

MATE   Aye, aye, sir. [*He goes out hurriedly. A moment later there is the sound of scuffling feet from the deck outside and the* MATE'S *voice shouting orders.*]

KEENEY [*Speaking aloud to himself—derisively*] And I was agoin' home like a yaller dog!

MRS. KEENEY [*Imploringly*]   David!

KEENEY [*Sternly*]   Woman, you ain't adoin' right when you meddle in men's business and weaken 'em. You can't know my feelin's. I got to prove a man to be a good husband for ye to take pride in. I got to git the ile, I tell ye.

MRS KEENEY [*Supplicatingly*]   David! Aren't you going home?

KEENEY [*Ignoring this question—commandingly*]
You ain't well. Go and lay down a mite. [*He starts
for the door.*] I got to git on deck. [*He goes out. She
cries after him in anguish*] David! [*A pause. She
passes her hand across her eyes—then commences to
laugh hysterically and goes to the organ. She sits
down and starts to play wildly an old hymn. KEENEY
reënters from the doorway to the deck and stands
looking at her angrily. He comes over and grabs her
roughly by the shoulder.*]

KEENEY Woman, what foolish mockin' is this?
[*She laughs wildly and he starts back from her in
alarm.*] Annie! What is it? [*She doesn't answer him.
KEENEY's voice trembles.*] Don't you know me,
Annie? [*He puts both hands on her shoulders and
turns her around so that he can look into her eyes.
She stares up at him with a stupid expression, a
vague smile on her lips. He stumbles away from her,
and she commences softly to play the organ again.*]

KEENEY [*Swallowing hard—in a hoarse whisper,
as if he had difficulty in speaking*] You said—you
was a-goin' mad—God! [*A long wail is heard from
the deck above.*] Ah bl-o-o-o-ow! [*A moment later
the MATE's face appears through the skylight. He
cannot see MRS. KEENEY.*]

MATE [*In great excitement*] Whales, sir—a whole
school of 'em—off the star'b'd quarter 'bout five mile
away—big ones!

KEENEY [*Galvanized into action*] Are you lower-
in' the boats?

MATE Yes, sir.

KEENEY [*With grim decision*]　I'm a-comin' with ye.

MATE　Aye, aye, sir. [*Jubilantly*] You'll git the ile now right enough, sir. [*His head is withdrawn and he can be heard shouting orders.*]

KEENEY [*Turning to his wife*]　Annie! Did you hear him? I'll git the ile. [*She doesn't answer or seem to know he is there. He gives a hard laugh, which is almost a groan.*] I know you're foolin' me, Annie. You ain't out of your mind—[*Anxiously*] be you? I'll git the ile now right enough—jest a little while longer, Annie—then we'll turn hom'ard. I can't turn back now, you see that, don't ye? I've got to git the ile. [*In sudden terror*] Answer me! You ain't mad, be you? [*She keeps on playing the organ, but makes no reply. The* MATE's *face appears again through the skylight.*]

MATE　All ready, sir. [KEENEY *turns his back on his wife and strides to the doorway, where he stands for a moment and looks back at her in anguish, fighting to control his feelings.*]

MATE　Comin', sir?

KEENEY [*His face suddenly grown hard with determination*]　Aye. [*He turns abruptly and goes out.* MRS. KEENEY *does not appear to notice his departure. Her whole attention seems centered in the organ. She sits with half-closed eyes, her body swaying a little from side to side to the rhythm of the hymn. Her fingers move faster and faster and she is playing wildly and discordantly as*

[*The curtain falls.*]

WHERE THE CROSS IS MADE

IS MADE

A Play in One Act

CHARACTERS

CAPTAIN ISAIAH BARTLETT
NAT BARTLETT, *his son*
SUE BARTLETT, *his daughter*
DOCTOR HIGGINS
SILAS HORNE, *mate*
CATES, *bosun*
JIMMY KANAKA, *harpooner*

of the schooner
Mary Allen

WHERE THE CROSS
IS MADE

SCENE *Captain Bartlett's "cabin"—a room erected as a lookout post at the top of his house situated on a high point of land on the California coast. The inside of the compartment is fitted up like the captain's cabin of a deep-sea sailing vessel. On the left, forward, a port-hole. Farther back, the stairs of the companionway. Still farther, two more portholes. In the rear, left, a marble-topped sideboard with a ship's lantern on it. In the rear, center, a door opening on stairs which lead to the lower house. A cot with a blanket is placed against the wall to the right of the door. In the right wall, five portholes. Directly under them, a wooden bench. In front of the bench, a long table with two straight-backed chairs, one in front, the other to the left of it. A cheap, dark-colored rug is on the floor. In the ceiling, midway from front to rear, a skylight extending from opposite the door to above the left edge of the table. In the right ex-*

*tremity of the skylight is placed a floating
ship's compass. The light from the binnacle
sheds over this from above and seeps down
into the room, casting a vague globular
shadow of the compass on the floor.*

*The time is an early hour of a clear windy
night in the fall of the year 1900. Moonlight,
winnowed by the wind which moans in the
stubborn angles of the old house, creeps
wearily in through the portholes and rests
like tired dust in circular patches upon the
floor and table. An insistent monotone of
thundering surf, muffled and far-off, is borne
upward from the beach below.*

*After the curtain rises the door in the rear
is opened slowly and the head and shoulders
of* NAT BARTLETT *appear over the sill. He
casts a quick glance about the room, and seeing no one there, ascends the remaining steps
and enters. He makes a sign to some one in
the darkness beneath: "All right, Doctor."*
DOCTOR HIGGINS *follows him into the room
and, closing the door, stands looking with
great curiosity around him. He is a slight,
medium-sized professional-looking man of
about thirty-five.* NAT BARTLETT *is very tall,
gaunt, and loose-framed. His right arm has
been amputated at the shoulder and the
sleeve on that side of the heavy mackinaw he
wears hangs flabbily or flaps against his body
as he moves. He appears much older than his
thirty years. His shoulders have a weary stoop*

as if worn down by the burden of his massive head with its heavy shock of tangled black hair. His face is long, bony, and sallow, with deep-set black eyes, a large aquiline nose, a wide thin-lipped mouth shadowed by an unkempt bristle of mustache. His voice is low and deep with a penetrating, hollow, metallic quality. In addition to the mackinaw, he wears corduroy trousers stuffed down into high laced boots.

NAT Can you see, Doctor?

HIGGINS [*In the too-casual tones which betray an inward uneasiness*] Yes—perfectly—don't trouble. The moonlight is so bright——

NAT Luckily. [*Walking slowly toward the table*] He doesn't want any light—lately—only the one from the binnacle there.

HIGGINS He? Ah—you mean your father?

NAT [*Impatiently*] Who else?

HIGGINS [*A bit startled—gazing around him in embarrassment*] I suppose this is all meant to be like a ship's cabin?

NAT Yes—as I warned you.

HIGGINS [*In surprise*] Warned me? Why warned? I think it's very natural—and interesting—this whim of his.

NAT [*Meaningly*] Interesting, it may be.

HIGGINS And he lives up here, you said—never comes down?

NAT Never—for the past three years. My sister brings his food up to him. [*He sits down in the chair to the left of the table.*] There's a lantern on the sideboard there, Doctor. Bring it over and sit down. We'll make a light. I'll ask your pardon for bringing you to this room on the roof—but—no one'll hear us here; and by seeing for yourself the mad way he lives—— Understand that I want you to get all the facts—just that, facts!—and for that light is necessary. Without that—they become dreams up here—dreams, Doctor.

HIGGINS [*With a relieved smile carries over the lantern*] It is a trifle spooky.

NAT [*Not seeming to notice this remark*] He won't take any note of this light. His eyes are too busy—out there. [*He flings his left arm in a wide gesture seaward.*] And if he does notice—well, let him come down. You're bound to see him sooner or later. [*He scratches a match and lights the lantern.*]

HIGGINS Where is—he?

NAT [*Pointing upward*] Up on the poop. Sit down, man! He'll not come—yet awhile.

HIGGINS [*Sitting gingerly on the chair in front of table*] Then he has the roof too rigged up like a ship?

NAT I told you he had. Like a deck, yes. A wheel, compass, binnacle light, the companionway there [*He points*], a bridge to pace up and down on —*and keep watch*. If the wind wasn't so high you'd hear him now—back and forth—all the live-long night. [*With a sudden harshness*] Didn't I tell you he's mad?

HIGGINS [*With a professional air*] That was nothing new. I've heard that about him from all

sides since I first came to the asylum yonder. You
say he only walks at night—up there?

NAT Only at night, yes. [*Grimly*] The things he
wants to see can't be made out in daylight—dreams
and such.

HIGGINS But just what is he trying to see? Does
any one know? Does he tell?

NAT [*Impatiently*] Why, every one knows what
Father looks for, man! The ship, of course.

HIGGINS What ship?

NAT His ship—the *Mary Allen*—named for my
dead mother.

HIGGINS But—I don't understand—— Is the ship
long overdue—or what?

NAT Lost in a hurricane off the Celebes with all
on board—three years ago!

HIGGINS [*Wonderingly*] Ah. [*After a pause*] But
your father still clings to a doubt——

NAT There is no doubt for him or any one else
to cling to. She was sighted bottom up, a complete
wreck, by the whaler John Slocum. That was two
weeks after the storm. They sent a boat out to read
her name.

HIGGINS And hasn't your father ever heard——

NAT He was the first to hear, naturally. Oh, he
knows right enough, if that's what you're driving at.
[*He bends toward the doctor—intensely.*] He *knows*,
Doctor, he *knows*—but he won't *believe*. He can't—
and keep living.

HIGGINS [*Impatiently*] Come, Mr. Bartlett, let's
get down to brass tacks. You didn't drag me up here
to make things more obscure, did you? Let's have

the facts you spoke of. I'll need them to give sympathetic treatment to his case when we get him to the asylum.

NAT [Anxiously—lowering his voice] And you'll come to take him away to-night—for sure?

HIGGINS Twenty minutes after I leave here I'll be back in the car. That's positive.

NAT And you know your way through the house?

HIGGINS Certainly, I remember—but I don't see——

NAT The outside door will be left open for you. You must come right up. My sister and I will be here—with him. And you understand—— Neither of us knows anything about this. The authorities have been complained to—not by us, mind—but by some one. He must never know——

HIGGINS Yes, yes—but still I don't—— Is he liable to prove violent?

NAT No—no. He's quiet always—too quiet; but he might do something—anything—if he knows——

HIGGINS Rely on me not to tell him, then; but I'll bring along two attendants in case—— [He breaks off and continues in matter-of-fact tones.] And now for the facts in this case, if you don't mind, Mr. Bartlett.

NAT [Shaking his head—moodily] There are cases where facts—— Well, here goes—the brass tacks. My father was a whaling captain as his father before him. The last trip he made was seven years ago. He expected to be gone two years. It was four before we saw him again. His ship had been wrecked in the Indian Ocean. He and six others managed to reach a small island on the fringe of the Archipelago—an island barren as hell, Doctor—after seven days in an open boat. The rest of the whaling crew never were heard from again—gone to the sharks. Of the six who reached the island with my father only three were alive when a fleet of Malay canoes picked them up, mad from thirst and starvation, the four of them. These four men finally reached Frisco. [*With great emphasis*] They were my father; Silas Horne, the mate; Cates, the bosun, and Jimmy Kanaka, a Hawaiian harpooner. Those four! [*With a forced laugh*] There are facts for you. It was all in the papers at the time—my father's story.

HIGGINS But what of the other three who were on the island?

NAT [*Harshly*] Died of exposure, perhaps. Mad and jumped into the sea, perhaps. That was the told story. Another was whispered—killed and eaten, perhaps! But gone—vanished—that, undeniably. That was the fact. For the rest—who knows? And what does it matter?

HIGGINS [*With a shudder*] I should think it would matter—a lot.

NAT [*Fiercely*] We're dealing with facts, Doctor! [*With a laugh*] And here are some more for you. My father brought the three down to this house with him—Horne and Cates and Jimmy Kanaka. We hardly recognized my father. He had been through hell and looked it. His hair was white. But you'll see for yourself—soon. And the others—they were all a bit queer, too—mad, if you will. [*He laughs again.*]

So much for the facts, Doctor. They leave off there and the dreams begin.

HIGGINS [*Doubtfully*] It would seem—the facts are enough.

NAT Wait. [*He resumes deliberately.*] One day my father sent for me and in the presence of the others told me the dream. I was to be heir to the secret. Their second day on the island, he said, they discovered in a sheltered inlet the rotten, water-logged hulk of a Malay prau—a proper war prau such as the pirates used to use. She had been there rotting—God knows how long. The crew had vanished—God knows where, for there was no sign on the island that man had ever touched there. The Kanakas went over the prau—they're devils for staying under water, you know—and they found—in two chests—[*He leans back in his chair and smiles ironically*]—Guess what, Doctor?

HIGGINS [*With an answering smile*] Treasure, of course.

NAT [*Leaning forward and pointing his finger accusingly at the other*] You see! The root of belief is in you, too! [*Then he leans back with a hollow chuckle.*] Why, yes. Treasure, to be sure. What else? They landed it and—you can guess the rest, too— diamonds, emeralds, gold ornaments—innumerable, of course. Why limit the stuff of dreams? Ha-ha! [*He laughs sardonically as if mocking himself.*]

HIGGINS [*Deeply interested*] And then?

NAT They began to go mad—hunger, thirst, and the rest—and they began to forget. Oh, they forgot a lot, and lucky for them they did, probably. But my father realizing, as he told me, what was happening to them, insisted that while they still knew what they were doing they should—guess again now, Doctor. Ha-ha!

HIGGINS   Bury the treasure?

NAT [*Ironically*] Simple, isn't it? Ha-ha. And then they made a map—the same old dream, you see—with a charred stick, and my father had care of it. They were picked up soon after, mad as hatters, as I have told you, by some Malays. [*He drops his mocking and adopts a calm, deliberate tone again.*] But the map isn't a dream, Doctor. We're coming back to facts again. [*He reaches into the pocket of his mackinaw and pulls out a crumpled paper.*] Here. [*He spreads it out on the table.*]

HIGGINS [*Craning his neck eagerly*] Dammit! This is interesting. The treasure, I suppose, is where——

NAT   Where the cross is made.

HIGGINS   And here are the signatures, I see. And that sign?

NAT   Jimmy Kanaka's. He couldn't write.

HIGGINS   And below? That's yours, isn't it?

NAT   As heir to the secret, yes. We all signed it here the morning the *Mary Allen,* the schooner my father had mortgaged this house to fit out, set sail to bring back the treasure. Ha-ha.

HIGGINS   The ship he's still looking for—that was lost three years ago?

NAT   The *Mary Allen,* yes. The other three men sailed away on her. Only father and the mate knew the approximate location of the island—and I—as heir. It's—— [*He hesitates, frowning.*] No matter. I'll keep the mad secret. My father wanted to go with them—but my mother was dying. I dared not go either.

HIGGINS Then you wanted to go? You believed in the treasure then?

NAT Of course. Ha-ha. How could I help it? I believed until my mother's death. Then *he* became mad, entirely mad. He built this cabin—to wait in— and he suspected my growing doubt as time went on. So, as final proof, he gave me a thing he had kept hidden from them all—a sample of the richest of the treasure. Ha-ha. Behold! [*He takes from his pocket a heavy bracelet thickly studded with stones and throws it on the table near the lantern.*]

HIGGINS [*Picking it up with eager curiosity—as if in spite of himself*] Real jewels?

NAT Ha-ha! You want to believe, too. No—paste and brass—Malay ornaments.

HIGGINS You had it looked over?

NAT Like a fool, yes. [*He puts it back in his pocket and shakes his head as if throwing off a burden.*] Now you know why he's mad—waiting for that ship—and why in the end I had to ask you to take him away where he'll be safe. The mortgage— the price of that ship—is to be foreclosed. We have to move, my sister and I. We can't take him with us. She is to be married soon. Perhaps away from the sight of the sea he may——

HIGGINS [*Perfunctorily*] Let's hope for the best.

And I fully appreciate your position. [*He gets up, smiling.*] And thank you for the interesting story. I'll know how to humor him when he raves about treasure.

NAT [*Somberly*] He is quiet always—too quiet. He only walks to and fro—watching——

HIGGINS Well, I must go. You think it's best to take him to-night?

NAT [*Persuasively*] Yes, Doctor. The neighbors—they're far away but—for my sister's sake—you understand.

HIGGINS I see. It must be hard on her—this sort of thing—Well—[*He goes to the door, which* NAT *opens for him.*] I'll return presently. [*He starts to descend.*]

NAT [*Urgently*] Don't fail us, Doctor. And come right up. He'll be here. [*He closes the door and tiptoes carefully to the companionway. He ascends it a few steps and remains for a moment listening for some sound from above. Then he goes over to the table, turning the lantern very low, and sits down, resting his elbows, his chin on his hands, staring somberly before him. The door in the rear is slowly opened. It creaks slightly and* NAT *jumps to his feet—in a thick voice of terror.*] Who's there? [*The door swings wide open, revealing* SUE BARTLETT. *She ascends into the room and shuts the door behind her. She is a tall, slender woman of twenty-five, with a pale, sad face framed in a mass of dark red hair. This hair furnishes the only touch of color about her. Her full lips are pale; the blue of her wistful wide eyes is fading into a twilight gray. Her voice is low and melancholy. She wears a dark wrapper and slippers.*]

SUE [*Stands and looks at her brother accusingly*] It's only I. What are you afraid of?

NAT [*Averts his eyes and sinks back on his chair again*] Nothing. I didn't know—I thought you were in your room.

SUE [*Comes to the table*] I was reading. Then I heard some one come down the stairs and go out. Who was it? [*With sudden terror*] It wasn't—Father?

NAT No. He's up there—watching—as he always is.

SUE [*Sitting down—insistently*] Who was it?

NAT [*Evasively*] A man—I know.

SUE What man? What is he? You're holding something back. Tell me.

NAT [*Raising his eyes defiantly*] A doctor.

SUE [*Alarmed*] Oh! [*With quick intuition*] You brought him up here—so that I wouldn't know!

NAT [*Doggedly*] No. I took him up here to see how things were—to ask him about Father.

SUE [*As if afraid of the answer she will get*] Is he one of them—from the asylum? Oh, Nat, you haven't——

NAT [*Interrupting her—hoarsely*] No, no! Be still.

SUE That would be—the last horror.

NAT [*Defiantly*] Why? You always say that. What could be more horrible than things as they are? I believe—it would be better for him—away—

where he couldn't see the sea. He'll forget his mad idea of waiting for a lost ship and a treasure that never was. [*As if trying to convince himself—vehemently*] I believe this!

SUE [*Reproachfully*] You don't, Nat. You know he'd die if he hadn't the sea to live with.

NAT [*Bitterly*] And you know old Smith will foreclose the mortgage. Is that nothing? We cannot pay. He came yesterday and talked with me. He knows the place is his—to all purposes. He talked as if we were merely his tenants, curse him! And he swore he'd foreclose immediately unless——

SUE [*Eagerly*] What?

NAT [*In a hard voice*] Unless we have—Father—taken away.

SUE [*In anguish*] Oh! But why, why? What is Father to him?

NAT The value of the property—our home which is his, Smith's. The neighbors are afraid. They pass by on the road at nights coming back to their farms from the town. They see *him* up there walking back and forth—waving his arms against the sky. They're afraid. They talk of a complaint. They say for his own good he must be taken away. They even whisper the house is haunted. Old Smith is afraid of his property. He thinks that *he* may set fire to the house—do anything——

SUE [*Despairingly*] But you told him how foolish that was, didn't you? That Father is quiet, always quiet.

NAT What's the use of telling—when they believe—when they're afraid? [SUE *hides her face in her hands—a pause—*NAT *whispers hoarsely*] I've been afraid myself—at times.

SUE   Oh, Nat! Of what?

NAT [*Violently*]   Oh, him and the sea he calls to! Of the damned sea he forced me on as a boy— the sea that robbed me of my arm and made me the broken thing I am!

SUE [*Pleadingly*]   You can't blame Father—for your misfortune.

NAT   He took me from school and forced me on his ship, didn't he? What would I have been now but an ignorant sailor like him if he had had his way? No. It's the sea I should not blame, that foiled him by taking my arm and then throwing me ashore —another one of *his* wrecks!

SUE [*With a sob*]   You're bitter, Nat—and hard. It was so long ago. Why can't you forget?

NAT [*Bitterly*]   Forget! You can talk! When Tom comes home from this voyage you'll be married and out of this with life before you—a captain's wife as our mother was. I wish you joy.

SUE [*Supplicatingly*]   And you'll come with us, Nat—and Father, too—and then——

NAT   Would you saddle your young husband with a madman and a cripple? [*Fiercely*] No, no, not I! [*Vindictively*] And not him, either! [*With sudden meaning—deliberately*] I've got to stay here. My book is three-fourths done—my book that will set me free! But I know, I feel, as sure as I stand here living before you, that I must finish it here. It could not live for me outside of this house where it was born. [*Staring at her fixedly*] So I will stay—in spite of hell! [SUE *sobs hopelessly. After a pause he continues*] Old Smith told me I could live here indefinitely without paying—as caretaker—if——

SUE [*Fearfully—like a whispered echo*] If?

NAT [*Staring at her—in a hard voice*] If I have *him* sent—where he'll no longer harm himself—nor others.

SUE [*With horrified dread*] No—no, Nat! For our dead mother's sake.

NAT [*Struggling*] Did I say I had? Why do you look at me—like that?

SUE Nat! Nat! For our mother's sake!

NAT [*In terror*] Stop! Stop! She's dead—and at peace. Would you bring her tired soul back to him again to be bruised and wounded?

SUE Nat!

NAT [*Clutching at his throat as though to strangle something within him—hoarsely*] Sue! Have mercy! [*His sister stares at him with dread foreboding.* NAT *calms himself with an effort and continues deliberately*] Smith said he would give two thousand cash if I would sell the place to him—and he would let me stay, rent free, as caretaker.

SUE [*Scornfully*] Two thousand! Why, over and over the mortgage its worth——

NAT It's not what it's worth. It's what one can get, cash—for my book—for freedom!

SUE So that's why he wants Father sent away, the wretch! He must know the will Father made——

NAT Gives the place to me. Yes, he knows. I told him.

SUE [*Dully*] Ah, how vile men are!

NAT [*Persuasively*] If it were to be done—if it were, I say—there'd be half for you for your wedding portion. That's fair.

SUE [*Horrified*] Blood money! Do you think I could touch it?

NAT [*Persuasively*] It would be only fair. I'd give it you.

SUE My God, Nat, are you trying to bribe me?

NAT No. It's yours in all fairness. [*With a twisted smile*] You forget I'm heir to the treasure, too, and can afford to be generous. Ha-ha.

SUE [*Alarmed*] Nat! You're so strange. You're sick, Nat. You couldn't talk this way if you were yourself. Oh, we must go away from here—you and Father and I! Let Smith foreclose. There'll be something over the mortgage; and we'll move to some little house—by the sea so that Father——

NAT [*Fiercely*] Can keep up his mad game with me—whispering dreams in my ear—pointing out to sea—mocking me with stuff like this! [*He takes the bracelet from his pocket. The sight of it infuriates him and he hurls it into a corner, exclaiming in a terrible voice*] No! No! It's too late for dreams now. It's too late! I've put them behind me to-night— forever!

SUE [*Looks at him and suddenly understands that what she dreads has come to pass—letting her head fall on her outstretched arms with a long moan*] Then—you've done it! You've sold him! Oh, Nat, you're cursed!

NAT [*With a terrified glance at the roof above*]

Ssshh! What are you saying? He'll be better off—away from the sea.

SUE [*Dully*] You've sold him.

NAT [*Wildly*] No! No! [*He takes the map from his pocket.*] Listen, Sue! For God's sake, listen to me! See! The map of the island. [*He spreads it out on the table.*] And the treasure—where the cross is made. [*He gulps and his words pour out incoherently.*] I've carried it about for years. Is that nothing? You don't know what it means. It stands between me and my book. It's stood between me and life—driving me mad! *He* taught me to wait and hope with him—wait and hope—day after day. He made me doubt my brain and give the lie to my eyes—when hope was dead—when I knew it was all a dream—I couldn't kill it! [*His eyes starting from his head*] God forgive me, I still believe! And that's mad—mad, do you hear?

SUE [*Looking at him with horror*] And that is why—you hate him!

NAT No, I don't—— [*Then in a sudden frenzy*] Yes! I do hate him! He's stolen my brain! I've got to free myself, can't you see, from him—and his madness.

SUE [*Terrified—appealingly*] Nat! Don't! You talk as if——

NAT [*With a wild laugh*] As if I were mad? You're right—but I'll be mad no more! See! [*He opens the lantern and sets fire to the map in his hand. When he shuts the lantern again it flickers and goes out. They watch the paper burn with fascinated eyes as he talks.*] See how I free myself and

become sane. And now for facts, as the doctor said.
I lied to you about him. He was a doctor from the
asylum. See how it burns! It must all be destroyed—
this poisonous madness. Yes, I lied to you—see—it's
gone—the last speck—and the only other map is the
one Silas Horne took to the bottom of the sea with
him. [*He lets the ash fall to the floor and crushes it
with his foot.*] Gone! I'm free of it—at last! [*His face
is very pale, but he goes on calmly.*] Yes, I sold him,
if you will—to save my soul. They're coming from
the asylum to get him—— [*There is a loud, muffled
cry from above, which sounds like "Sail-ho," and a
stamping of feet. The slide to the companionway
above is slid back with a bang. A gust of air tears
down into the room.* NAT *and* SUE *have jumped to
their feet and stand petrified.* CAPTAIN BARTLETT
tramps down the stairs.]

NAT [*With a shudder*]   God! Did he hear?

SUE   Ssshh! [CAPTAIN BARTLETT *comes into the
room. He bears a striking resemblance to his son,
but his face is more stern and formidable, his form
more robust, erect and muscular. His mass of hair
is pure white, his bristly mustache the same, con-
trasting with the weather-beaten leather color of his
furrowed face. Bushy gray brows overhang the ob-
sessed glare of his fierce dark eyes. He wears a heavy,
double-breasted blue coat, pants of the same mate-
rial, and rubber boots turned down from the knee.*]

BARTLETT [*In a state of mad exultation strides
toward his son and points an accusing finger at him.*
NAT *shrinks backward a step.*]   Bin thinkin' me
mad, did ye? Thinkin' it for the past three years, ye

bin—ever since them fools on the *Slocum* tattled their damn lie o' the *Mary Allen* bein' a wreck.

NAT [*Swallowing hard—chokingly*] No—Father—I——

BARTLETT Don't lie, ye whelp! You that I'd made my heir—aimin' to git me out o' the way! Aimin' to put me behind the bars o' the jail for mad folk!

SUE Father—no!

BARTLETT [*Waving his hand for her to be silent*] Not you, girl, not you. You're your mother.

NAT [*Very pale*] Father—do you think—I——

BARTLETT [*Fiercely*] A lie in your eyes! I bin a-readin' 'em. My curse on you!

SUE Father! Don't!

BARTLETT Leave me be, girl. He believed, didn't he? And ain't he turned traitor—mockin' at me and sayin' it's all a lie—mockin' at himself, too, for bein' a fool to believe in dreams, as he calls 'em.

NAT [*Placatingly*] You're wrong, Father. I do believe.

BARTLETT [*Triumphantly*] Aye, now ye do! Who wouldn't credit their own eyes?

NAT [*Mystified*] Eyes?

BARTLETT Have ye not seen her, then? Did ye not hear me hail?

NAT [*Confusedly*] Hail? I heard a shout. But—hail what?—seen what?

BARTLETT [*Grimly*] Aye, now's your punishment, Judas. [*Explosively*] The *Mary Allen*, ye blind fool, come back from the Southern Seas—come back as I swore she must!

SUE [*Trying to soothe him*] Father! Be quiet.
It's nothing.

BARTLETT [*Not heeding her—his eyes fixed hyp-
notically on his son's*] Turned the pint a half-hour
back—the *Mary Allen*—loaded with gold as I swore
she would be—carryin' her lowers—not a reef in 'em
—makin' port, boy, as I swore she must—too late for
traitors, boy, too late!—droppin' her anchor just
when I hailed her.

NAT [*A haunted, fascinated look in his eyes,
which are fixed immovably on his father's*] The
Mary Allen! But how do you know?

BARTLETT Not know my own ship! 'Tis you're
mad!

NAT But at night—some other schooner——

BARTLETT No other, I say! The *Mary Allen*—
clear in the moonlight. And heed this: D'you call to
mind the signal I gave to Silas Horne if he made
this port o' a night?

NAT [*Slowly*] A red and a green light at the
mainmast-head.

BARTLETT [*Triumphantly*] Then look out if ye
dare! [*He goes to the porthole, left forward.*] Ye
can see it plain from here. [*Commandingly*] Will
ye believe your eyes? Look—and then call me mad!
[NAT *peers through the porthole and starts back,
a dumbfounded expression on his face.*]

NAT [*Slowly*] A red and a green at the mainmast-head. Yes—clear as day.

SUE [*With a worried look at him*] Let me see.
[*She goes to the porthole.*]

BARTLETT [*To his son with fierce satisfaction*]

Aye, ye see now clear enough—too late for you [NAT *stares at him spellbound.*] And from above I saw Horne and Cates and Jimmy Kanaka plain on the deck in the moonlight lookin' up at me. Come! [*He strides to the companionway, followed by* NAT. *The two of them ascend.* SUE *turns from the port-hole, an expression of frightened bewilderment on her face. She shakes her head sadly. A loud "Mary Allen, ahoy!" comes from above in* BARTLETT'S *voice, followed like an echo by the same hail from* NAT. SUE *covers her face with her hands, shuddering.* NAT *comes down the companionway, his eyes wild and exulting.*]

SUE [*Brokenly*] He's bad to-night, Nat. You're right to humor him. It's the best thing.

NAT [*Savagely*] Humor him? What in hell do you mean?

SUE [*Pointing to the porthole*] There's nothing there, Nat. There's not a ship in harbor.

NAT You're a fool—or blind! The *Mary Allen's* there in plain sight of any one, with the red and the green signal lights. Those fools lied about her being wrecked. And I've been a fool, too.

SUE But, Nat, there's nothing. [*She goes over to the porthole again.*] Not a ship. See.

NAT I saw, I tell you! From above it's all plain. [*He turns from her and goes back to his seat by the table.* SUE *follows him, pleading frightenedly.*]

SUE Nat! You mustn't let this—— You're all excited and trembling, Nat. [*She puts a soothing hand on his forehead.*]

NAT [*Pushing her away from him roughly*] You

blind fool! [*Bartlett comes down the steps of the companionway. His face is transfigured with the ecstasy of a dream come true.*]

BARTLETT They've lowered a boat—the three—Horne and Cates and Jimmy Kanaka. They're a-rowin' ashore. I heard the oars in the locks. Listen! [*A pause*]

NAT [*Excitedly*] I hear!

SUE [*Who has taken the chair by her brother—in a warning whisper*] It's the wind and sea you hear, Nat. Please!

BARTLETT [*Suddenly*] Hark! They've landed. They're back on earth again as I swore they'd come back. They'll be a-comin' up the path now. [*He stands in an attitude of rigid attention. NAT strains forward in his chair. The sound of the wind and sea suddenly ceases and there is a heavy silence. A dense green glow floods slowly in rhythmic waves like a liquid into the room—as of great depths of the sea faintly penetrated by light.*]

NAT [*Catching at his sister's hand—chokingly*] See how the light changes! Green and gold! [*He shivers.*] Deep under the sea! I've been drowned for years! [*Hysterically*] Save me! Save me!

SUE [*Patting his hand comfortingly*] Only the moonlight, Nat. It hasn't changed. Be quiet, dear, it's nothing. [*The green light grows deeper and deeper.*]

BARTLETT [*In a crooning, monotonous tone*] They move slowly—slowly. They're heavy, I know, heavy—the two chests. Hark! They're below at the door. You hear?

NAT [*Starting to his feet*] I hear! I left the door open.

BARTLETT For them?

NAT For them.

SUE [*Shuddering*] Ssshh! [*The sound of a door being heavily slammed is heard from way down in the house.*]

NAT [*To his sister—excitedly*] There! You hear?

SUE A shutter in the wind.

NAT There is no wind.

BARTLETT Up they come! Up, bullies! They're heavy—heavy! [*The paddling of bare feet sounds from the floor below—then comes up the stairs.*]

NAT You hear them now?

SUE Only the rats running about. It's nothing, Nat.

BARTLETT [*Rushing to the door and throwing it open*] Come in, lads, come in!—and welcome home! [*The forms of* SILAS HORNE, CATES, *and* JIMMY KANAKA *rise noiselessly into the room from the stairs. The last two carry heavy inlaid chests.* HORNE *is a parrot-nosed, angular old man dressed in gray cotton trousers and a singlet torn open across his hairy chest.* JIMMY *is a tall, sinewy, bronzed young Kanaka. He wears only a breech cloth.* CATES *is squat and stout and is dressed in dungaree pants and a shredded white sailor's blouse, stained with iron rust. All are in their bare feet. Water drips from their soaked and rotten clothes. Their hair is matted, intertwined with slimy strands of seaweed. Their eyes, as they glide silently into the room, stare frightfully wide at nothing. Their flesh in the green light has the suggestion of decomposition. Their bodies sway limply, nervelessly, rhythmically as if to the pulse of long swells of the deep sea.*]

NAT [*Taking a step toward them*] See! [*Frenziedly*] Welcome home, boys!

SUE [*Grabbing his arm*] Sit down, Nat. It's nothing. There's no one there. Father—sit down!

BARTLETT [*Grinning at the three and putting his finger to his lips*] Not here, boys, not here—not before him. [*He points to his son.*] He has no right, now. Come. The treasure is ours only. We'll go away with it together. Come. [*He goes to the companionway. The three follow. At the foot of it* HORNE *puts a swaying hand on his shoulder and with the other holds out a piece of paper to him.* BARTLETT *takes it and chuckles exultantly.*] That's right—for him—that's right! [*He ascends. The figures sway up after him.*]

NAT [*Frenziedly*] Wait! [*He struggles toward the companionway.*]

SUE [*Trying to hold him back*] Nat—don't! Father—come back!

NAT   Father! [*He flings her away from him and rushes up the companionway. He pounds against the slide, which seems to have been shut down on him.*]

SUE [*Hysterically—runs wildly to the door in rear*] Help! Help! [*As she gets to the door* DOCTOR HIGGINS *appears, hurrying up the stairs.*]

HIGGINS [*Excitedly*] Just a moment, Miss. What's the matter?

SUE [*With a gasp*] My father—up there!

HIGGINS I can't see—where's my flash? Ah. [*He flashes it on her terror-stricken face, then quickly around the room. The green glow disappears. The wind and sea are heard again. Clear moonlight floods through the portholes.* HIGGINS *springs to the companionway.* NAT *is still pounding.*] Here, Bartlett. Let me try.

NAT [*Coming down—looking dully at the doctor*] They've locked it. I can't get up.

HIGGINS [*Looks up—in an astonished voice*] What's the matter, Bartlett? It's all open. [*He starts to ascend.*]

NAT [*In a voice of warning*] Look out, man! Look out for them!

HIGGINS [*Calls down from above*] Them? Who? There's no one here. [*Suddenly—in alarm.*] Come up! Lend a hand here! He's fainted! [NAT *goes up slowly.* SUE *goes over and lights the lantern, then hurries back to the foot of the companionway with it. There is a scuffling noise from above. They reappear, carrying* CAPTAIN BARTLETT'S *body.*]

HIGGINS Easy now! [*They lay him on the couch in rear.* SUE *sets the lantern down by the couch.* HIGGINS *bends and listens for a heart-beat. Then he rises, shaking his head.*] I'm sorry——

SUE [*Dully*] Dead?

HIGGINS [*Nodding*] Heart failure, I should judge. [*With an attempt at consolation*] Perhaps it's better so, if——

NAT [*As if in a trance*] There was something Horne handed him. Did you see?

SUE [*Wringing her hands*] Oh, Nat, be still!

He's dead. [*To* HIGGINS *with pitiful appeal*] Please go—go——

HIGGINS There's nothing I can do?

SUE Go—please—— [HIGGINS *bows stiffly and goes out.* NAT *moves slowly to his father's body, as if attracted by some irresistible fascination.*]

NAT Didn't you see? Horne handed him something.

SUE [*Sobbing*] Nat! Nat! Come away! Don't touch him, Nat! Come away. [*But her brother does not heed her. His gaze is fixed on his father's right hand, which hangs downward over the side of the couch. He pounces on it and forcing the clenched fingers open with a great effort, secures a crumpled ball of paper.*]

NAT [*Flourishing it above his head with a shout of triumph*] See! [*He bends down and spreads it out in the light of the lantern.* The map of the island! Look! It isn't lost for me after all! There's still a chance—*my* chance! [*With mad, solemn decision*] When the house is sold I'll go—and I'll find it! Look! It's written here in his handwriting: "The treasure is buried where the cross is made."

SUE [*Covering her face with her hands—brokenly*] Oh, God! Come away, Nat! Come away!

[*The curtain falls.*]

THE ROPE

A Play in One Act

CHARACTERS

ABRAHAM BENTLEY
ANNIE, *his daughter*
PAT SWEENEY, *her husband*
MARY, *their child*
LUKE BENTLEY, *Abe's son by a second marriage*

THE ROPE

SCENE *The interior of an old barn situated on top of a high headland of the seacoast. In the rear, to the left, a stall in which lumber is stacked up. To the right of it, an open double doorway looking out over the ocean. Outside the doorway, the faint trace of what was once a road leading to the barn. Beyond the road, the edge of a cliff which rises sheer from the sea below. On the right of the doorway, three stalls with mangers and hay-ricks. The first of these is used as a woodbin and is half full of piled-up cordwood. Near this bin, a chopping block with an ax driven into the top of it.*

The left section of the barn contains the hay loft, which extends at a height of about twelve feet from the floor as far to the right as the middle of the doorway. The loft is bare except for a few scattered mounds of dank-looking hay. From the edge of the loft, half way from the door, a rope about five feet long with an open running noose at the end is hanging. A rusty plow and various other farming implements, all giving evidence of long disuse, are lying on the floor near the left wall. Farther forward an old cane-bottomed chair is set back against the wall.

In front of the stalls on the right stands a long, roughly constructed carpenter's table, evidently home-made. Saws, a lathe, a hammer, chisel, a keg containing nails and other tools of the carpentry trade are on the table. Two benches are placed, one in front, one to the left of it.

The right side of the barn is a bare wall.

It is between six and half-past in the evening of a day in early spring. At the rising of the curtain some trailing clouds near the horizon, seen through the open doorway, are faintly tinged with gold by the first glow of the sunset. As the action progresses this reflected light gradually becomes brighter, and then slowly fades into a smoky crimson. The sea is a dark slate color. From the rocks below the headland sounds the muffled monotone of breaking waves.

As the curtain rises MARY is discovered squatting cross-legged on the floor, her back propped against the right side of the doorway, her face in profile. She is a skinny, over-grown girl of ten with thin, carroty hair worn in a pig-tail. She wears a shabby gingham dress. Her face is stupidly expression-

less. Her hands flutter about aimlessly in relaxed, flabby gestures.

She is staring fixedly at a rag doll which she has propped up against the doorway opposite her. She hums shrilly to herself.

At a sudden noise from outside she jumps to her feet, peeks out, and quickly snatches up the doll, which she hugs fiercely to her breast. Then, after a second's fearful hesitation, she runs to the carpenter's table and crawls under it.

As she does so ABRAHAM BENTLEY *appears in the doorway and stands, blinking into the shadowy barn. He is a tall, lean stoop-shouldered old man of sixty-five. His thin legs, twisted by rheumatism, totter feebly under him as he shuffles slowly along by the aid of a thick cane. His face is gaunt, chalky-white, furrowed with wrinkles, surmounted by a shiny bald scalp fringed with scanty wisps of white hair. His eyes peer weakly from beneath bushy, black brows. His mouth is a sunken line drawn in under his large, beak-like nose. A two weeks' growth of stubby patches of beard covers his jaws and chin. He has on a threadbare brown overcoat but wears no hat.*

BENTLEY [*Comes slowly into the barn, peering around him suspiciously. As he reaches the table and leans one hand on it for support,* MARY *darts from underneath and dashes out through the door-*

way. BENTLEY *is startled; then shakes his cane after her*] Out o' my sight, you Papist brat! Spawn o' Satan! Spyin' on me! They set her to it. Spyin' to watch me! [*He limps to the door and looks out cautiously. Satisfied, he turns back into the barn.*] Spyin' to see—what they'll never know. [*He stands staring up at the rope and taps it testingly several times with his stick, talking to himself as he does so.*] It's tied strong—strong as death—— [*He cackles with satisfaction.*] They'll see, then! They'll see! [*He laboriously creeps over to the bench and sits down wearily. He looks toward the sea and his voice quavers in a doleful chant*] "Woe unto us! for the day goeth away, for the shadows of the evening are stretched out." [*He mumbles to himself for a moment—then speaks clearly.*] Spyin' on me! Spawn o' the Pit! [*He renews his chant.*] "They hunt our steps that we cannot go in our streets: our end is near, our days are fulfilled; for our end is come."

[*As he finishes* ANNIE *enters. She is a thin, slovenly, worn-out looking woman of about forty with a drawn, pasty face. Her habitual expression is one of a dulled irritation. She talks in a high-pitched, sing-song whine. She wears a faded gingham dress and a torn sunbonnet.*]

ANNIE [*Comes over to her father but warily keeps out of range of his stick*] Paw! [*He doesn't answer or appear to see her.*] Paw! You ain't fergittin' what the doctor told you when he was here last, be you? He said you was to keep still and not go a-walkin' round. Come on back to the house, Paw.

It's gittin' near supper time and you got to take your medicine b'fore it, like he says.

BENTLEY [*His eyes fixed in front of him*] "The punishment of thine iniquity is accomplished, O daughter of Zion: he will visit thine iniquity, O daughter of Edom; he will discover thy sins."

ANNIE [*Waiting resignedly until he has finished—wearily*] You better take watch on your health, Paw, and not be sneakin' up to this barn no more. Lord sakes, soon 's ever my back is turned you goes sneakin' off agen. It's enough to drive a body outa their right mind.

BENTLEY "Behold, every one that useth proverbs shall use this proverb against thee, saying, As is the mother, so is her daughter!" [*He cackles to himself*] So is her daughter!

ANNIE [*Her face flushing with anger*] And if I am, I'm glad I take after her and not you, y'old wizard! [*Scornfully*] A fine one you be to be shoutin' Scripture in a body's ears all the live-long day— you that druv Maw to her death with your naggin', and pinchin', and miser stinginess. If you've a mind to pray, it's down in the medder you ought to go, and kneel down by her grave, and ask God to forgive you for the meanness you done to her all her life.

BENTLEY [*Mumbling*] "As is the mother, so is her daughter."

ANNIE [*Enraged by the repetition of this quotation*] *You* quotin' Scripture! Why, Maw wasn't cold in the earth b'fore you was down in the port courtin' agen—courtin' that harlot that was the talk

o' the whole town! And then you disgraces yourself
and me by marryin' her—*her*—and bringin' her back
home with you; and me still goin' every day to put
flowers on Maw's grave that you'd fergotten. [*She
glares at him vindictively, pausing for breath.*] And
between you you'd have druv me into the grave like
you done Maw if I hadn't married Pat Sweeney
so's I could git away and live in peace. Then you
took on so high and mighty 'cause he was a Cath'lic
—*you* gittin' religion all of a moment just for spite
on me 'cause I'd left—and b'cause she egged you on
against me; *you* sayin' it was a sin to marry a Papist,
after not bein' at Sunday meetin' yourself for
more'n twenty years!

BENTLEY [*Loudly*] "He will visit thine iniquity—"

ANNIE [*Interrupting*] And the carryin's-on you
had the six years at home after I'd left you—the
shame of the whole county! Your wife, indeed with
a child she *claimed* was your'n, and her goin' with
this farmer and that, and even men off the ships in
the port, and you blind to it! And then when she
got sick of you and ran away—only to meet her end
at the hands of God a year after—she leaves you
alone with that—*your* son, Luke, *she* called him—
and him only five years old!

BENTLEY [*Babbling*] Luke? Luke?

ANNIE [*Tauntingly*] Yes, Luke! "As is the
mother, so is her son"—that's what you ought to
preach 'stead of puttin' curses on me. You was glad
enough to git me back home agen, and Pat with
me, to tend the place, and help bring up that brat
of hers. [*Jealously*] You was fond enough of him

all them years—and how did he pay you back? Stole
your money and ran off and left you just when he
was sixteen and old enough to help. Told you to
your face he'd stolen and was leavin'. He only
laughed when you was took crazy and cursed him;
and he only laughed harder when you hung up
that silly rope there [*She points*] and told him to
hang himself on it when he ever came home agen.

BENTLEY [*Mumbling*] You'll see, then. You'll
see!

ANNIE [*Wearily—her face becoming dull and
emotionless again*] I s'pose I'm a bigger fool than
you be to argy with a half-witted body. But I tell
you agen that Luke of yours ain't comin' back;
and if he does he ain't the kind to hang himself,
more's the pity. He's like her. He'd hang *you* more
likely if he s'pected you had any money. So you
might 's well take down that ugly rope you've had
tied there since he run off. He's probably dead
anyway by this.

BENTLEY [*Frightened*] No! No!

ANNIE Them as bad as him comes to a sudden
end. [*Irritably*] Land sakes, Paw, here I am
argyin' with your lunatic notions and the supper
not ready. Come on and git your medicine. You can
see no one ain't touched your old rope. Come on!
You can sit 'n' read your Bible. [*He makes no movement. She comes closer to him and peers into his
face—uncertainly.*] Don't you hear me? I do hope
you ain't off in one of your fits when you don't
know nobody. D'you know who's talkin'? This is
Annie—your Annie, Paw.

BENTLEY [*Bursting into senile rage*] None o' mine! Spawn o' the Pit! [*With a quick movement he hits her viciously over the arm with his stick. She gives a cry of pain and backs away from him, holding her arm.*]

ANNIE [*Weeping angrily*] That's what I git for tryin' to be kind to you, you ugly old devil! [*The sound of a man's footsteps is heard from outside, and* SWEENEY *enters. He is a stocky, muscular, sandy-haired Irishman dressed in patched corduroy trousers shoved down into high laced boots, and a blue flannel shirt. The bony face of his bullet head has a pressed-in appearance except for his heavy jaw, which sticks out pugnaciously. There is an expression of mean cunning and cupidity about his mouth and his small, round, blue eyes. He has evidently been drinking and his face is flushed and set in an angry scowl.*]

SWEENEY Have ye no supper at all made, ye lazy slut? [*Seeing that she has been crying*] What're you blubberin' about?

ANNIE It's all his fault. I was tryin' to git him home but he's that set I couldn't budge him; and he hit me on the arm with his cane when I went near him.

SWEENEY He did, did he? I'll soon learn him better. [*He advances toward* BENTLEY *threateningly.*]

ANNIE [*Grasping his arm*] Don't touch him, Pat. He's in one of his fits and you might kill him.

SWEENEY An' good riddance!

BENTLEY [*Hissing*] Papist! [*Chants*] "Pour out

thy fury upon the heathen that know thee not, and
upon the families that call not on thy name: for
they have eaten up Jacob, and devoured him, and
consumed him, and made his habitation desolate."

SWEENEY [*Instinctively crosses himself—then
scornfully*] Spit curses on me till ye choke. It's not
likely the Lord God'll be listenin' to a wicked auld
sinner the like of you. [*To* ANNIE] What's got into
him to be roamin' up here? When I left for the
town he looked too weak to lift a foot.

ANNIE Oh, it's the same crazy notion he's had
ever since Luke left. He wanted to make sure the
rope was still here.

BENTLEY [*Pointing to the rope with his stick*]
He-he! Luke'll come back. Then you'll see. You'll
see!

SWEENEY [*Nervously*] Stop that mad cacklin'
for the love of heaven! [*With a forced laugh*] It's
great laughter I should be havin' at you, mad as
you are, for thinkin' that thief of a son of yours
would come back to hang himself on account of
your curses. It's five years he's been gone, and not
a sight of him; an' you, cursin' an' callin' down the
wrath o' God on him by day an' by night. That
shows you what God thinks of your curses—an' Him
deaf to you!

ANNIE It's no use talkin' to him, Pat.

SWEENEY I've small doubt but that Luke is hung
long since—by the police. He's come to no good
end, that lad. [*His eyes on the rope*] I'll be pullin'
that thing down, so I will; an' the auld loon'll
stay in the house, where he belongs, then, maybe.

[*He reaches up for the rope as if to try and yank it down.* BENTLEY *waves his stick frantically in the air, and groans with rage.*]

ANNIE [*Frightened*]   Leave it alone, Pat. Look at him. He's liable to hurt himself. Leave his rope be. It don't do no harm.

SWEENEY [*Reluctantly moves away*]   It looks ugly hangin' there open like a mouth. [*The old man sinks back into a relieved immobility.* SWEENEY *speaks to his wife in a low tone.*] Where's the child? Get her to take him out o' this. I want a word with you he'll not be hearin'. [*She goes to the door and calls out*] Ma-ry! Ma-ry! [*A faint, answering cry is heard and a moment later* MARY *rushes breathlessly into the barn.* SWEENEY *grabs her roughly by the arm. She shrinks away, looking at him with terrified eyes.*] You're to take your grandfather back to the house—an' see to it he stays there.

ANNIE   And give him his medicine.

SWEENEY [*As the child continues to stare at him silently with eyes stupid from fear, he shakes her impatiently*]   D'you hear me now? [*To his wife*] It's soft-minded she is, like I've always told you, an' stupid; and you're not too firm in the head yourself at times, God help you! An' look at him! It's the curse is in the wits of your family, not mine.

ANNIE   You've been drinkin' in town or you wouldn't talk that way.

MARY [*Whining*]   Maw! I'm skeered!

SWEENEY [*Lets go of her arm and approaches* BENTLEY]   Get up out o' this, ye auld loon, an' go with Mary. She'll take you to the house. [BENTLEY *tries to hit him with the cane.*] Oho, ye would, would ye? [*He wrests the cane from the old man's hands.*] Bad cess to ye, you're the treach'rous one! Get up, now! [*He jerks the old man to his feet.*] Here, Mary, take his hand. Quick now! [*She does so tremblingly.*] Lead him to the house.

ANNIE   Go on, Paw! I'll come and git your supper in a minute.

BENTLEY [*Stands stubbornly and begins to intone*]   "O Lord, thou hast seen my wrong; judge thou my cause. Thou hast seen all their **vengeance** and all their imaginations against me——"

SWEENEY [*Pushing him toward the door.* BENTLEY *tries to resist.* MARY *pulls at his hand in a sudden fit of impish glee, and laughs shrilly.*]   Get on now an' stop your cursin'.

BENTLEY   "Render unto them a recompense, O Lord, according to the work of their hands."

SWEENEY   Shut your loud quackin'! Here's your cane. [*He gives it to the old man as they come to the doorway and quickly steps back out of reach.*] An' mind you don't touch the child with it or I'll beat you to a jelly, old as ye are.

BENTLEY [*Resisting* MARY's *efforts to pull him out, stands shaking his stick at* SWEENEY *and his wife*]   "Give them sorrow of heart, thy curse unto them. Persecute and destroy them in anger from under the heavens of the Lord."

MARY [*Tugging at his hand and bursting again into shrill laughter*]   Come on, Gran'paw. [*He allows himself to be led off, right.*]

SWEENEY [*Making the sign of the cross furtively—*

with a sigh of relief] He's gone, thank God! What a snake's tongue he has in him! [*He sits down on the bench to the left of table.*] Come here, Annie, till I speak to you. [*She sits down on the bench in front of table.* SWEENEY *winks mysteriously.*] Well, I saw him, sure enough.

ANNIE [*Stupidly*] Who?

SWEENEY [*Sharply*] Who? Who but Dick Waller, the lawyer, that I went to see. [*Lowering his voice*] An' I've found out what we was wishin' to know. [*With a laugh*] Ye said I'd been drinkin'—which is true; but 'twas all in the plan I'd made. I've a head for strong drink, as ye know, but he hasn't. [*He winks cunningly.*] An' the whiskey loosened his tongue till he'd told all he knew.

ANNIE He told you—about Paw's will?

SWEENEY He did. [*Disappointedly*] But for all the good it does us we might as well be no wiser than we was before. [*He broods for a moment in silence—then hits the table furiously with his fist.*] God's curse on the auld miser!

ANNIE What did he tell you?

SWEENEY Not much at the first. He's a cute one, an' he'd be askin' a fee to tell you your own name, if he could get it. His practice is all dribbled away from him lately on account of the drink. So I let on I was only payin' a friendly call, havin' known him for years. Then I asked him out to have a drop o' drink, knowin' his weakness; an' we had rashers of them, an' I payin' for it. Then I come out with it straight and asked him about the will—because the auld man was crazy an' on his last legs, I told him, an' he was the lawyer made out the will when Luke was gone. So he winked at me an' grinned—he was drunk by this—an' said: "It's no use, Pat. He left the farm to the boy." "To hell with the farm," I spoke back. "It's mortgaged to the teeth; but how about the money?" "The money?" an' he looks at me in surprise, "What money?" "The cash he has," I says. "You're crazy," he says. "There wasn't any cash—only the farm." "D'you mean to say he made no mention of money in his will?" I asked. You could have knocked me down with a feather. "He did not—on my oath," he says. [SWEENEY *leans over to his wife—indignantly.*] Now what d'you make o' that? The auld divil!

ANNIE Maybe Waller was lyin'.

SWEENEY He was not. I could tell by his face. He was surprised to hear me talkin' of money.

ANNIE But the thousand dollars Paw got for the mortgage just before that woman ran away——

SWEENEY An' that I've been slavin' me hands off to pay the int'rist on!

ANNIE What could he have done with that? He ain't spent it. It was in twenty-dollar gold pieces he got it, I remember Mr. Kellar of the bank tellin' me once.

SWEENEY Divil a penny he's spent. Ye know as well as I do if it wasn't for my hammerin', an' sawin', an' nailin', he'd be in the poor house this minute—or the mad house, more likely.

ANNIE D'you suppose that harlot ran off with it?

SWEENEY I do not; I know better—an' so do you.

D'you not remember the letter she wrote tellin'
him he could support Luke on the money he'd got
on the mortgage she'd signed with him; for he'd
made the farm over to her when he married her.
An' where d'you suppose Luke got the hundred
dollars he stole? The auld loon must have had cash
with him then, an' it's only five years back.

ANNIE He's got it hid some place in the house
most likely.

SWEENEY Maybe you're right. I'll dig in the
cellar this night when he's sleepin'. He used to be
down there a lot recitin' Scripture in his fits.

ANNIE What else did Waller say?

SWEENEY Nothin' much; except that we should
put notices in the papers for Luke, an' if he didn't
come back by sivin years from when he'd left—two
years from now, that'd be—the courts would say he
was dead an' give us the farm. Divil a lot of use it
is to us now with no money to fix it up; an' himself
ruinin' it years ago by sellin' everythin' to buy that
slut new clothes.

ANNIE Don't folks break wills like his'n in the
courts?

SWEENEY Waller said 'twas no use. The auld
divil was plain in his full senses when he made it;
an' the courts cost money.

ANNIE [Resignedly] There ain't nothin' we can
do then.

SWEENEY No—except wait an' pray that young
thief is dead an' won't come back; an' try an' find
where it is the auld man has the gold hid, if he has
it yet. I'd take him by the neck an' choke him till

he told it, if he wasn't your father. [*He takes a full quart flask of whiskey from the pocket of his coat and has a big drink.*] Aahh! If we'd on'y the thousand we'd stock the farm good an' I'd give up this dog's game [*He indicates the carpentry outfit scornfully*] an' we'd both work hard with a man or two to help, an' in a few years we'd be rich; for 'twas always a payin' place in the auld days.

ANNIE Yes, yes, it was always a good farm then.

SWEENEY He'll not last long in his senses, the doctor told me. His next attack will be very soon an' after it he'll be a real lunatic with no legal claims to anythin'. If we on'y had the money—— 'Twould be the divil an' all if the auld fool should forget where he put it, an' him takin' leave of his senses altogether. [*He takes another nip at the bottle and puts it back in his pocket—with a sigh.*] Ah, well, I'll save what I can an' at the end of two years, with good luck in the trade, maybe we'll have enough. [*They are both startled by the heavy footsteps of some one approaching outside. A shrill burst of MARY's laughter can be heard and the deep voice of a man talking to her.*]

SWEENEY [*Uneasily*] It's Mary; but who could that be with her? It's not himself. [*As he finishes speaking LUKE appears in the doorway, holding the dancing MARY by the hand. He is a tall, strapping young fellow about twenty-five with a coarse-featured, rather handsome face bronzed by the sun. What his face lacks in intelligence is partly forgiven for his good-natured, half-foolish grin, his hearty laugh, his curly dark hair, a certain devil-may-care recklessness and irresponsible youth in voice and gesture. But his mouth is weak and characterless; his brown eyes are large but shifty and acquisitive. He wears a dark blue jersey, patched blue pants, rough sailor shoes, and a gray cap. He advances into the stable with a mocking smile on his lips until he stands directly under the rope. The man and woman stare at him in petrified amazement.*]

ANNIE   Luke!

SWEENEY [*Crossing himself*]   Glory be to God—it's him!

MARY [*Hopping up and down wildly*]   It's Uncle Luke, Uncle Luke, Uncle Luke! [*She runs to her mother, who pushes her away angrily.*]

LUKE [*Regarding them both with an amused grin*]   Sure, it's `Luke—back after five years of bummin' round the rotten old earth in ships and things. Paid off a week ago—had a bust-up—and then took a notion to come out here—bummed my way—and here I am. And you're both of you tickled to death to see me, ain't yuh?—like hell! [*He laughs and walks over to* ANNIE.] Don't yuh even want to shake flippers with your dear, long-lost brother, Annie? I remember you and me used to git on so fine together—like hell!

ANNIE [*Giving him a venomous look of hatred*]   Keep your hands to yourself.

LUKE [*Grinning*]   You ain't changed, that's sure—on'y yuh're homlier'n ever. [*He turns to the scowling Sweeney.*]   How about you, brother Pat?

SWEENEY   I'd not lower myself to take the hand of a——

LUKE [*With a threat in his voice*] Easy goes with that talk! I'm not so soft to lick as I was when I was a kid; and don't forget it.

ANNIE [*To* MARY, *who is playing catch with a silver dollar which she has had clutched in her hand—sharply*] Mary! What have you got there? Where did you get it? Bring it here to me this minute! [MARY *presses the dollar to her breast and remains standing by the doorway in stubborn silence.*]

LUKE Aw, let her alone! What's bitin' yuh? That's on'y a silver dollar I give her when I met her front of the house. She told me you was up here; and I give her that as a present to buy candy with. I got it in Frisco—cart-wheels, they call 'em. There ain't none of them in these parts I ever seen, so I brung it along on the voyage.

ANNIE [*Angrily*] I don't know or care where you got it—but I know you ain't come by it honest. Mary! Give that back to him this instant! [*As the child hesitates, she stamps her foot furiously.*] D'you hear me? [MARY *starts to cry softly, but comes to* LUKE *and hands him the dollar.*]

LUKE [*Taking it—with a look of disgust at his half-sister*] I was right when I said you ain't changed, Annie. You're as stinkin' mean as ever. [*To* MARY, *consolingly*] Quit bawlin', kid. You 'n' me'll go out on the edge of the cliff here and chuck some stones in the ocean same's we useter, remember? [MARY's *tears immediately cease. She looks up at him with shining eyes, and claps her hands.*]

MARY [*Pointing to the dollar he has in his hand*] Throw that! It's flat 'n' it'll skip.

LUKE [*With a grin*] That's the talk, kid. That's all it's good for—to throw away; not buryin' it like your miser folks'd tell you. Here! You take it and chuck it away. It's your'n. [*He gives her the dollar and she hops to the doorway. He turns to* PAT *with a grin.*] I'm learnin' your kid to be a sport, Tight-Wad. I hope you ain't got no objections.

MARY [*Impatiently*] Come on, Uncle Luke. Watch me throw it.

LUKE Aw right. [*To* PAT] I'll step outside a second and give you two a chanct to git all the dirty things yuh're thinkin' about me off your chest. [*Threateningly*] And then I'm gointer come and talk turkey to you, see? I didn't come back here for fun, and the sooner you gets that in your beans, the better.

MARY Come on and watch me!

LUKE Aw right, I'm comin'. [*He walks out and stands, leaning his back against the doorway, left.* MARY *is about six feet beyond him on the other side of the road. She is leaning down, peering over the edge of the cliff and laughing excitedly.*]

MARY Can I throw it now? Can I?

LUKE Don't git too near the edge, kid. The water's deep down there, and you'd be a drowned rat if you slipped. [*She shrinks back a step.*] You chuck it when I say three. Ready, now! [*She draws back her arm.*] One! Two! Three! [*She throws the dollar away and bends down to see it hit the water.*]

MARY [*Clapping her hands and laughing*] I

seen it! I seen it splash! It's deep down now, ain't it?

LUKE Yuh betcher it is! Now watch how far I kin chuck rocks. [*He picks up a couple and goes to where she is standing. During the following conversation between* SWEENEY *and his wife he continues to play this way with* MARY. *Their voices can be heard but the words are indistinguishable.*]

SWEENEY [*Glancing apprehensively toward the door—with a great sigh*] Speak of the divil an' here he is! [*Furiously*] Flingin' away dollars, the dirty thief, an' us without——

ANNIE (*Interrupting him*] Did you hear what he said? A thief like him ain't come back for no good. [*Lowering her voice*] D'you s'pose he knows about the farm bein' left to him?

SWEENEY [*Uneasily*] How could he? An' yet—I dunno—[*With sudden decision*] You'd best lave him to me to watch out for. It's small sense you have to hide your hate from him. You're as looney as the rist of your breed. An' he needs to be blarneyed round to fool him an' find out what he's wantin'. I'll pritind to make friends with him, God roast his soul! An' do you run to the house an' break the news to the auld man; for if he seen him suddin it's likely the little wits he has left would leave him; an' the thief could take the farm from us to-morrow if himself turned a lunatic.

ANNIE [*Getting up*] I'll tell him a little at a time till he knows.

SWEENEY Be careful, now, or we'll lose the farm this night. [*She starts towards the doorway.* SWEENEY

speaks suddenly in a strange, awed voice] Did you
see Luke when he first came in to us? He stood
there with the noose of the rope almost touchin'
his head. I was almost wishin'—— [*He hesitates.*]

ANNIE [*Viciously*] I was wishin' it was round his
neck chokin' him, that's what I was—hangin' him
just as Paw says.

SWEENEY Ssshh! He might hear ye. Go along,
now. He's comin' back.

MARY [*Pulling at* LUKE's *arm as he comes back
to the doorway*] Lemme throw 'nother! Lemme
throw 'nother!

LUKE [*Enters just as* ANNIE *is going out and stops
her*] Goin' to the house? Do we get any supper?
I'm hungry.

ANNIE [*Glaring at him but restraining her rage*]
Yes.

LUKE [*Jovially*] Good work! And tell the old
man I'm here and I'll see him in a while. He'll be
glad to see me, too—like hell! [*He comes forward.*
ANNIE *goes off, right.*]

MARY [*In an angry whine, tugging at his hand*]
Lemme throw 'nother. Lemme——

LUKE [*Shaking her away*] There's lots of rocks,
kid. Throw them. Dollars ain't so plentiful.

MARY [*Screaming*] No! No! I don' wanter throw
rocks. Lemme throw 'nother o' them.

SWEENEY [*Severely*] Let your uncle in peace, ye
brat! [*She commences to cry.*] Run help your mother
now or I'll give ye a good hidin'. [MARY *runs out of
the door, whimpering.* PAT *turns to* LUKE *and holds
out his hand.*]

LUKE [*Looking at it in amazement*] Ahoy, there! What's this?

SWEENEY [*With an ingratiating smile*] Let's let by-gones be by-gones. I'm harborin' no grudge agen you these past years. Ye was only a lad when ye ran away an' not to be blamed for it. I'd have taken your hand a while back, an' glad to, but for her bein' with us. She has the divil's own tongue, as ye know, an' she can't forget the rowin' you an' her used to be havin'.

LUKE [*Still looking at* SWEENEY'S *hand*] So that's how the wind blows! [*With a grin*] Well, I'll take a chanct. [*They shake hands and sit down by the table,* SWEENEY *on the front bench and* LUKE *on the left one.*]

SWEENEY [*Pulls the bottle from his coat pocket —with a wink*] Will ye have a taste? It's real stuff.

LUKE Yuh betcher I will! [*He takes a big gulp and hands the bottle back.*]

SWEENEY [*After taking a drink himself, puts bottle on table*] I wasn't wishin' herself to see it or I'd have asked ye sooner. [*There is a pause, during which each measures the other with his eyes.*]

LUKE Say, how's the old man now?

SWEENEY [*Cautiously*] Oh, the same as ivir— older an' uglier, maybe.

LUKE I thought he might be in the bug-house by this time.

SWEENEY [*Hastily*] Indeed not; he's foxy to pritind he's looney, but he's his wits with him all the time.

LUKE [*Insinuatingly*] Is he as stingy with his coin as he used to be?

SWEENEY If he owned the ocean he wouldn't give a fish a drink; but I doubt if he's any money left at all. Your mother got rid of it all, I'm thinkin'. [LUKE *smiles a superior, knowing smile.*] He has on'y the farm, an' that mortgaged. I've been payin' the int'rist an' supportin' himself an' his doctor's bills by the carpentryin' these five years past.

LUKE [*With a grin*] Huh! Yuh're slow. Yuh oughter get wise to yourself.

SWEENEY [*Inquisitively*] What d'ye mean by that?

LUKE [*Aggravatingly*] Aw, nothin'. [*He turns around and his eyes fix themselves on the rope.*] What the hell—— [*He is suddenly convulsed with laughter and slaps his thigh.*] Hahaha! If that don't beat the Dutch! The old nut!

SWEENEY What?

LUKE That rope. Say, has he had that hangin' there ever since I skipped?

SWEENEY [*Smiling*] Sure; an' he thinks you'll be comin' home to hang yourself.

LUKE Hahaha! Not this chicken! And you say he ain't crazy! Gee, that's too good to keep. I got to have a drink on that. [SWEENEY *pushes the bottle toward him. He raises it toward the rope.*] Here's how, old chum! [*He drinks.* SWEENEY *does likewise.*] Say, I'd a'most forgotten about that. Remember how hot he was that day when he hung that rope up and cussed me for pinchin' the hundred? He was

standin' there shakin' his stick at me, and I was
laughin' 'cause he looked so funny with the spit
dribblin' outa his mouth like he was a mad dog.
And when I turned round and beat it he shouted
after me: "Remember, when you come home again
there's a rope waitin' for yuh to hang yourself on,
yuh bastard!" [*He spits contemptuously.*] What a
swell chanct. [*His manner changes and he frowns.*]
The old slave-driver! That's a hell of a fine old
man for a guy to have!

SWEENEY [*Pushing the bottle toward him*]   Take
a sup an' forget it. 'Twas a long time past.

LUKE   But the rope's there yet, ain't it? And he
keeps it there. [*He takes a large swallow.* SWEENEY
also drinks.] But I'll git back at him aw right, yuh
wait 'n' see. I'll git every cent he's got this time.

SWEENEY [*Slyly*]   If he has a cent. I'm not wishful
to discourage ye, but—— [*He shakes his head doubtfully, at the same time fixing* LUKE *with a keen
glance out of the corner of his eye.*]

LUKE [*With a cunning wink*]   Aw, he's got it
aw right. You watch me! [*He is beginning to show
the effects of the drink he has had. He pulls out
tobacco and a paper and rolls a cigarette and lights
it. As he puffs he continues boastfully*] You country jays oughter wake up and see what's goin' on.
Look at me. I was green as grass when I left here,
but bummin' round the world, and bein' in cities,
and meetin' all kinds, and keepin' your two eyes
open—that's what'll learn yuh a cute trick or two.

SWEENEY   No doubt but you're right. Us country folks is stupid in most ways. We've no chance to learn the things a travelin' lad like you'd be knowin'.

LUKE [*Complacently*] Well, you watch me and I'll learn yuh. [*He snickers.*] So yuh think the old man's flat broke, do yuh?

SWEENEY I do so.

LUKE Then yoh're simple; that's what—simple! You're lettin' him kid yuh.

SWEENEY If he has any, it's well hid, I know that. He's a sly old bird.

LUKE And I'm a slyer bird. D'yuh hear that? I c'n beat his game any time. You watch me! [*He reaches out his hand for the bottle. They both drink again. SWEENEY begins to show signs of getting drunk. He hiccoughs every now and then and his voice grows uncertain and husky.*]

SWEENEY It'd be a crafty one who'd find where he'd hidden it, sure enough.

LUKE You watch me! I'll find it. I betcher anything yuh like I find it. You watch me! Just wait till he's asleep and I'll show yuh—ter-night. [*There is a noise of shuffling footsteps outside and ANNIE's whining voice raised in angry protest.*]

SWEENEY Ssshh! It's himself comin' now. [*LUKE rises to his feet and stands, waiting in a defensive attitude, a surly expression on his face. A moment later BENTLEY appears in the doorway, followed by ANNIE. He leans against the wall, in an extraordinary state of excitement, shaking all over, gasping for breath, his eyes devouring LUKE from head to foot.*]

ANNIE I couldn't do nothin' with him. When I told him *he'd* come back there was no holdin' him. He was a'most frothin' at the mouth till I let him out. [*Whiningly*] You got to see to him, Pat, if you want any supper. I can't——

SWEENEY Shut your mouth! We'll look after him.

ANNIE See that you do. I'm goin' back. [*She goes off, right. LUKE and his father stand looking at each other. The surly expression disappears from LUKE'S face, which gradually expands in a broad grin.*]

LUKE [*Jovially*] Hello, old sport! I s'pose yuh're tickled to pieces to see me—like hell! [*The old man stutters and stammers incoherently as if the very intensity of his desire for speech had paralyzed all power of articulation. LUKE turns to PAT.*] I see he ain't lost the old stick. Many a crack on the nut I used to get with that.

BENTLEY [*Suddenly finding his voice—chants*] "Bring forth the best robe, and put it on him; and put a ring on his hand, and shoes on his feet: And bring hither the fatted calf, and kill it; and let us eat, and be merry: For this my son was dead, and is alive again; he was lost, and is found." [*He ends up with a convulsive sob.*]

LUKE [*Disapprovingly*] Yuh're still spoutin' the rotten old Word o' God same's ever, eh? Say, give us a rest on that stuff, will yuh? Come on and shake hands like a good sport. [*He holds out his hand. The old man totters over to him, stretching out a trembling hand.* LUKE *seizes it and pumps it up and down.*] That's the boy!

SWEENEY [*Genuinely amazed*] Look at that, would ye--the two-faced auld liar. [BENTLEY *passes his trembling hand all over* LUKE, *feeling of his arms, his chest, his back. An expression of overwhelming joy suffuses his worn features.*]

LUKE [*Grinning at* SWEENEY] Say, watch this. [*With tolerant good-humor*] On the level I b'lieve the old boy's glad to see me at that. He looks like he was tryin' to grin; and I never seen him grin in my life, I c'n remember. [*As* BENTLEY *attempts to feel of his face*] Hey, cut it out! [*He pushes his hand away, but not roughly.*] I'm all here, yuh needn't worry. Yuh needn't be scared I'm a ghost. Come on and sit down before yuh fall down. Yuh ain't got your sea-legs workin' right. [*He guides the old man to the bench at left of table.*] Squat here for a spell and git your wind. [BENTLEY *sinks down on the bench.* LUKE *reaches for the bottle.*] Have a drink to my makin' port. It'll buck yuh up.

SWEENEY [*Alarmed*] Be careful, Luke. It might likely end him.

LUKE [*Holds the bottle up to the old man's mouth, supporting his head with the other hand.* BENTLEY *gulps, the whiskey drips over his chin, and he goes into a fit of convulsive coughing.* LUKE *laughs*] Hahaha! Went down the wrong way, did it? I'll show yuh the way to do it. [*He drinks.*] There yuh are—smooth as silk. [*He hands the bottle to* SWEENEY, *who drinks and puts it back on the table.*]

SWEENEY He must be glad to see ye or he'd not drink. 'Tis dead against it he's been these five years past. [*Shaking his head*] An' him cursin' you day an' night! I can't put head or tail to it. Look out he ain't meanin' some bad to ye underneath. He's crafty at pretendin'.

LUKE [*As the old man makes signs to him with his hand*] What's he after now? He's lettin' on he's lost his voice again. What d'yuh want? [BENTLEY *points with his stick to the rope. His lips move convulsively as he makes a tremendous effort to utter words.*]

BENTLEY [*Mumbling incoherently*] Luke—Luke —rope—Luke—hang.

SWEENEY [*Appalled*] There ye are! What did I tell you? It's to see you hang yourself he's wishin', the auld fiend!

BENTLEY [*Nodding*] Yes—Luke—hang.

LUKE [*Taking it as a joke—with a loud guffaw*] Hahaha! If that don't beat the Dutch! The old nanny-goat! Aw right, old sport. Anything to oblige. Hahaha! [*He takes the chair from left and places it under the rope. The old man watches him with eager eyes and seems to be trying to smile.* LUKE *stands on the chair.*]

SWEENEY Have a care, now! I'd not be foolin' with it in your place.

LUKE All out for the big hangin' of Luke Bentley by hisself. [*He puts the noose about his neck with an air of drunken bravado and grins at his father. The latter makes violent motions for him to go on.*] Look at him, Pat. By God, he's in a hurry.

Hahaha! Well, old sport, here goes nothin'. [*He makes a movement as if he were going to jump and kick the chair from under him.*]

SWEENEY [*Half starts to his feet—horrified*] Luke! Are ye gone mad?

LUKE [*Stands staring at his father, who is still making gestures for him to jump. A scowl slowly replaces his good-natured grin.*] D'yuh really mean it—that yuh want to see me hangin' myself? [BENTLEY *nods vigorously in the affirmative.* LUKE *glares at him for a moment in silence.*] Well, I'll be damned! [*To* PAT] An' I thought he was only kiddin'. [*He removes the rope gingerly from his neck. The old man stamps his foot and gesticulates wildly, groaning with disappointment.* LUKE *jumps to the floor and looks at his father for a second. Then his face grows white with a vicious fury.*] I'll fix your hash, you stinkin' old murderer! [*He grabs the chair by its back and swings it over his head as if he were going to crush* BENTLEY'S *skull with it. The old man cowers on the bench in abject terror.*]

SWEENEY [*Jumping to his feet with a cry of alarm*] Luke! For the love of God! [LUKE *hesitates; then hurls the chair in back of him under the loft, and stands menacingly in front of his father, his hands on his hips.*]

LUKE [*Grabbing* BENTLEY'S *shoulder and shaking him—hoarsely*] Yuh wanted to see me hangin' there in real earnest, didn't yuh? You'd hang me yourself if yuh could, wouldn't yuh? And you my own father! Yuh damned son of a gun! Yuh would, would yuh? I'd smash your brains out for a nickel!

[*He shakes the old man more and more furiously.*]

SWEENEY Luke! Look out! You'll be killin'
him next.

LUKE [*Giving his father one more shake, which
sends him sprawling on the floor*] Git outa here!
Git outa this b'fore I kill yuh dead! [SWEENEY
rushes over and picks the terrified old man up.]
Take him outa here, Pat! [*His voice rises to a
threatening roar.*] Take him outa here or I'll break
every bone in his body! [*He raises his clenched fists
over his head in a frenzy of rage.*]

SWEENEY Ssshh! Don't be roarin'! I've got him.
[*He steers the whimpering, hysterical* BENTLEY *to
the doorway.*] Come out o' this, now. Get down to
the house! Hurry now! Ye've made enough trouble
for one night. [*They disappear off right.* LUKE
*flings himself on a bench, breathing heavily. He
picks up the bottle and takes a long swallow.*
SWEENEY *reënters from rear. He comes over and sits
down in his old place.*] Thank God he's off down to
the house, scurryin' like a frightened hare as if he'd
never a kink in his legs in his life. He was moanin'
out loud so you could hear him a long ways. [*With
a sigh.*] It's a murd'rous auld loon he is, sure
enough.

LUKE [*Thickly*] The damned son of a gun!

SWEENEY I thought you'd be killin' him that
time with the chair.

LUKE [*Violently*] Serve him damn right if I
done it.

SWEENEY An' you laughin' at him a moment
sooner! I thought 'twas jokin' ye was.

LUKE [*Sullenly*]   So I was kiddin'; but I thought
he was tryin' to kid me, too. And then I seen by
the way he acted he really meant it. [*Banging the
table with his fist*] Ain't that a hell of a fine old
man for yuh!

SWEENEY   He's a mean auld swine.

LUKE   He meant it aw right, too. Yuh shoulda
seen him lookin' at me. [*With sudden lugubrious-
ness*] Ain't he a hell of a nice old man for a guy to
have? Ain't he?

SWEENEY [*Soothingly*]   Hush! It's all over now.
Don't be thinkin' about it.

LUKE [*On the verge of drunken tears*]   How kin
I help thinkin'—and him my own father? After me
bummin' and starvin' round the rotten earth, and
workin' myself to death on ships and things—and
when I come home he tries to make me bump off—
wants to see me a corpse—my own father, too! Ain't
he a hell of an old man to have? The rotten son of
a gun!

SWEENEY   It's past an' done. Ferget it. [*He
slaps* LUKE *on the shoulder and pushes the bottle
toward him.*] Let's take a drop more. We'll be
goin' to supper soon.

LUKE [*Takes a big drink—huskily*]   Thanks. [*He
wipes his mouth on his sleeve with a snuffle.*] But
I'll tell yuh something you can put in your pipe
and smoke. It ain't past and done, an' it ain't
goin' to be! [*More and more aggressively*] And I
ain't goin' to ferget it, either! Yuh kin betcher life
on that, pal. And *he* ain't goin' to ferget it—not
if he lives a million—not by a damned sight! [*With*

sudden fury] I'll fix his hash! I'll git even with him, the old skunk! You watch me! And this very night, too!

SWEENEY   How d'you mean?

LUKE   You just watch me, I tell yuh! [*Banging the table*] I said I'd git even and I will git even—this same night, with no long waits, either! [*Frowning*] Say, you don't stand up for him, do yuh?

SWEENEY   [*Spitting—vehemently*] That's child's talk. There's not a day passed I've not wished him in his grave.

LUKE   [*Excitedly*] Then we'll both git even on him—you 'n' me. We're pals, ain't we?

SWEENEY   Sure.

LUKE   And yuh kin have half what we gits. That's the kinda feller I am! That's fair enough, ain't it?

SWEENEY   Surely.

LUKE   I don't want no truck with this rotten farm. You kin have my share of that. I ain't made to be no damned dirt puncher—not me! And I ain't goin' to loaf round here more'n I got to, and when I goes this time I ain't never comin' back. Not me! Not to punch dirt and milk cows. You kin have the rotten farm for all of me. What I wants is cash—regular coin yuh kin spend—not dirt. I want to show the gang a real time, and then ship away to sea agen or go bummin' agen. I want coin yuh kin throw away—same's your kid chucked that dollar of mine overboard, remember? A real dollar, too! She's a sport, aw right!

SWEENEY   [*Anxious to bring him back to the*

subject] But where d'you think to find his money?

LUKE [*Confidently*] Don't yuh fret. I'll show
yuh. You watch me! I know his hidin' places. I
useter spy on him when I was a kid—— Maw used
to make me—and I seen him many a time at his
sneakin'. [*Indignantly*] He used to hide stuff from
the old lady. What d'yuh know about him—the
mean skunk.

SWEENEY That was a long time back. You don't
know——

LUKE [*Assertively*] But I do know, see! He's
got two places. One was where I swiped the hundred.

SWEENEY It'll not be there, then.

LUKE No; but there's the other place; and he
never knew I was wise to that. I'd have left him
clean on'y I was a kid and scared to pinch more.
So you watch me! We'll git even on him, you 'n'
me, and go halfs, and yuh kin start the rotten farm
goin' agen and I'll beat it where there's some life.

SWEENEY But if there's no money in that place,
what'll you be doin' to find out where it is, then?

LUKE Then you 'n' me 'ull make him tell!

SWEENEY Oho, don't think it! 'Tis not him'd be
tellin'.

LUKE Aw, say, you're simple! You watch me!
I know a trick or two about makin' people tell what
they don't wanter. [*He picks up the chisel from
the table.*] Yuh see this? Well, if he don't answer
up nice and easy we'll show him! [*A ferocious grin
settles over his face.*] We'll git even on him, you 'n'
me—and he'll tell where it's hid. We'll just shove

this into the stove till it's red hot and take off his shoes and socks and warm the bottoms of his feet for him. [*Savagely*] He'll tell then—anything we wants him to tell.

SWEENEY   But Annie?

LUKE   We'll shove a rag in her mouth so's she can't yell. That's easy.

SWEENEY [*His head lolling drunkenly—with a cruel leer*] 'Twill serve him right to heat up his hoofs for him, the limpin', auld miser!—if ye don't hurt him too much.

LUKE [*With a savage scowl*] We won't hurt him—more'n enough. [*Suddenly raging*] I'll pay him back aw right! He won't want no more people to hang themselves when I git through with him. I'll fix his hash! [*He sways to his feet, the chisel in his hand.*] Come on! Let's git to work. Sooner we starts the sooner we're rich. [SWEENEY *rises. He is steadier on his feet than* LUKE. *At this moment* MARY *appears in the doorway.*]

MARY   Maw says supper's ready. I had mine. [*She comes into the room and jumps up, trying to grab hold of the rope.*] Lift me, Uncle Luke. I wanter swing.

LUKE [*Severely*]   Don't yuh dare touch that rope, d'yuh hear?

MARY [*Whining*]   I wanter swing.

LUKE [*With a shiver*]   It's bad, kid. Yuh leave it alone, take it from me.

SWEENEY   She'll get a good whalin' if I catch her jumpin' at it.

LUKE Come on, pal. T'hell with supper. We got work to do first. [*They go to the doorway.*]

SWEENEY [*Turning back to the sulking Mary*] And you stay here, d'you hear, ye brat, till we call ye—or I'll skin ye alive.

LUKE And ter-morrer mornin', kid, I'll give yuh a whole handful of them shiny, bright things yuh chucked in the ocean—and yuh kin be a real sport.

MARY [*Eagerly*] Gimme 'em now! Gimme 'em now, Uncle Luke. [*As he shakes his head—whiningly*] Gimme one! Gimme one!

LUKE Can't be done, kid. Ter-morrer. Me 'n' your old man is goin' to git even now—goin' to make him pay for——

SWEENEY [*Interrupting—harshly*] Hist with your noise! D'you think she's no ears? Don't be talkin' so much. Come on, now.

LUKE [*Permitting himself to be pulled out the doorway*] Aw right! I'm with yuh. We'll git even —you 'n' me. The damned son of a gun! [*They lurch off to the right.*]

[MARY *skips to the doorway and peeps after them for a moment. Then she comes back to the center of the floor and looks around her with an air of decision. She sees the chair in under the loft and runs over to it, pulling it back and setting it on its legs directly underneath the noose of the rope. She climbs and stands on the top of the chair and grasps the noose with both her upstretched hands. Then with a shriek of delight she kicks the chair from under her and launches herself for a swing. The rope seems to part where it is fixed to the beam. A*

*dirty gray bag tied to the end of the rope falls to the
floor with a muffled, metallic thud.* MARY *sprawls
forward on her hands and knees, whimpering.
Straggly wisps from the pile of rank hay fall silently
to the floor in a mist of dust.* MARY, *discovering she
is unhurt, glances quickly around and sees the bag.
She pushes herself along the floor and, untying the
string at the top, puts in her hand. She gives an exclamation of joy at what she feels and, turning the
bag upside down, pours its contents in her lap. Giggling to herself, she gets to her feet and goes to the
doorway, where she dumps what she has in her lap
in a heap on the floor just inside the barn. They
lie there in a little glittering pile, shimmering in
the faint sunset glow—fifty twenty-dollar gold
pieces.* MARY *claps her hands and sings to herself:
"Skip—skip—skip." Then she quickly picks up four
or five of them and runs out to the edge of the cliff.
She throws them one after another into the ocean as
fast as she can and bends over to see them hit the
water. Against the background of horizon clouds
still tinted with blurred crimson she hops up and
down in a sort of grotesque dance, clapping her
hands and laughing shrilly. After the last one is
thrown she rushes back into the barn to get more.*]

MARY [*Picking up a handful—giggling ecstati-
cally*] Skip! Skip! [*She turns and runs out to throw
them as*

[*The curtain falls.*]

EUGENE O'NEILL was born on October 16, 1888, in New York City. His father was James O'Neill, the famous dramatic actor; and during his early years O'Neill traveled much with his parents. In 1909 he went on a gold-prospecting expedition to South America; he later shipped as a seaman to Buenos Aires, worked at various occupations in the Argentine and tended mules on a cattle steamer to South Africa. He returned to New York destitute, then worked briefly as a reporter on a newspaper in New London, Connecticut, at which point an attack of tuberculosis sent him for six months to a sanitarium. This event marked the turning point in his career, and shortly after, at the age of twenty-four, he began his first play. His major works include *The Emperor Jones,* 1920; *The Hairy Ape,* 1921; *Desire Under the Elms,* 1924; *The Great God Brown,* 1925; *Strange Interlude,* 1926, 1927; *Mourning Becomes Electra,* 1929, 1931; *Ah, Wilderness,* 1933; *Days Without End,* 1934; *A Moon for the Misbegotten,* 1945; *The Iceman Cometh,* 1946; and several plays produced posthumously, including *Long Day's Journey into Night, A Touch of the Poet* and *Hughie.* Eugene O'Neill died in 1953.

77696009 2